Mometrix
TEST PREPARATION

I0893678

DSST®

Criminal Justice
Exam Secrets
Study Guide

Dear Future Exam Success Story

First of all, **THANK YOU** for purchasing Mometrix study materials!

Second, congratulations! You are one of the few determined test-takers who are committed to doing whatever it takes to excel on your exam. **You have come to the right place.** We developed these study materials with one goal in mind: to deliver you the information you need in a format that's concise and easy to use.

In addition to optimizing your guide for the content of the test, we've outlined our recommended steps for breaking down the preparation process into small, attainable goals so you can make sure you stay on track.

We've also analyzed the entire test-taking process, identifying the most common pitfalls and showing how you can overcome them and be ready for any curveball the test throws you.

Standardized testing is one of the biggest obstacles on your road to success, which only increases the importance of doing well in the high-pressure, high-stakes environment of test day. Your results on this test could have a significant impact on your future, and this guide provides the information and practical advice to help you achieve your full potential on test day.

Your success is our success

We would love to hear from you! If you would like to share the story of your exam success or if you have any questions or comments in regard to our products, please contact us at **800-673-8175** or **support@mometrix.com**.

Thanks again for your business and we wish you continued success!

Sincerely,
The Mometrix Test Preparation Team

Need more help? Check out our flashcards at:
http://MometrixFlashcards.com/DSST

Written and edited by the Mometrix Exam Secrets Test Prep Team
Printed in the United States of America

TABLE OF CONTENTS

Introduction

Thank you for purchasing this resource! You have made the choice to prepare yourself for a test that could have a huge impact on your future, and this guide is designed to help you be fully ready for test day. Obviously, it's important to have a solid understanding of the test material, but you also need to be prepared for the unique environment and stressors of the test, so that you can perform to the best of your abilities.

For this purpose, the first section that appears in this guide is the **Secret Keys**. We've devoted countless hours to meticulously researching what works and what doesn't, and we've boiled down our findings to the five most impactful steps you can take to improve your performance on the test. We start at the beginning with study planning and move through the preparation process, all the way to the testing strategies that will help you get the most out of what you know when you're finally sitting in front of the test.

We recommend that you start preparing for your test as far in advance as possible. However, if you've bought this guide as a last-minute study resource and only have a few days before your test, we recommend that you skip over the first two Secret Keys since they address a long-term study plan.

If you struggle with **test anxiety**, we strongly encourage you to check out our recommendations for how you can overcome it. Test anxiety is a formidable foe, but it can be beaten, and we want to make sure you have the tools you need to defeat it.

Secret Key #1 – Plan Big, Study Small

There's a lot riding on your performance. If you want to ace this test, you're going to need to keep your skills sharp and the material fresh in your mind. You need a plan that lets you review everything you need to know while still fitting in your schedule. We'll break this strategy down into three categories.

Information Organization

Start with the information you already have: the official test outline. From this, you can make a complete list of all the concepts you need to cover before the test. Organize these concepts into groups that can be studied together, and create a list of any related vocabulary you need to learn so you can brush up on any difficult terms. You'll want to keep this vocabulary list handy once you actually start studying since you may need to add to it along the way.

Time Management

Once you have your set of study concepts, decide how to spread them out over the time you have left before the test. Break your study plan into small, clear goals so you have a manageable task for each day and know exactly what you're doing. Then just focus on one small step at a time. When you manage your time this way, you don't need to spend hours at a time studying. Studying a small block of content for a short period each day helps you retain information better and avoid stressing over how much you have left to do. You can relax knowing that you have a plan to cover everything in time. In order for this strategy to be effective though, you have to start studying early and stick to your schedule. Avoid the exhaustion and futility that comes from last-minute cramming!

Study Environment

The environment you study in has a big impact on your learning. Studying in a coffee shop, while probably more enjoyable, is not likely to be as fruitful as studying in a quiet room. It's important to keep distractions to a minimum. You're only planning to study for a short block of time, so make the most of it. Don't pause to check your phone or get up to find a snack. It's also important to **avoid multitasking**. Research has consistently shown that multitasking will make your studying dramatically less effective. Your study area should also be comfortable and well-lit so you don't have the distraction of straining your eyes or sitting on an uncomfortable chair.

The time of day you study is also important. You want to be rested and alert. Don't wait until just before bedtime. Study when you'll be most likely to comprehend and remember. Even better, if you know what time of day your test will be, set that time aside for study. That way your brain will be used to working on that subject at that specific time and you'll have a better chance of recalling information.

Finally, it can be helpful to team up with others who are studying for the same test. Your actual studying should be done in as isolated an environment as possible, but the work of organizing the information and setting up the study plan can be divided up. In between study sessions, you can discuss with your teammates the concepts that you're all studying and quiz each other on the details. Just be sure that your teammates are as serious about the test as you are. If you find that your study time is being replaced with social time, you might need to find a new team.

Secret Key #2 – Make Your Studying Count

You're devoting a lot of time and effort to preparing for this test, so you want to be absolutely certain it will pay off. This means doing more than just reading the content and hoping you can remember it on test day. It's important to make every minute of study count. There are two main areas you can focus on to make your studying count.

Retention

It doesn't matter how much time you study if you can't remember the material. You need to make sure you are retaining the concepts. To check your retention of the information you're learning, try recalling it at later times with minimal prompting. Try carrying around flashcards and glance at one or two from time to time or ask a friend who's also studying for the test to quiz you.

To enhance your retention, look for ways to put the information into practice so that you can apply it rather than simply recalling it. If you're using the information in practical ways, it will be much easier to remember. Similarly, it helps to solidify a concept in your mind if you're not only reading it to yourself but also explaining it to someone else. Ask a friend to let you teach them about a concept you're a little shaky on (or speak aloud to an imaginary audience if necessary). As you try to summarize, define, give examples, and answer your friend's questions, you'll understand the concepts better and they will stay with you longer. Finally, step back for a big picture view and ask yourself how each piece of information fits with the whole subject. When you link the different concepts together and see them working together as a whole, it's easier to remember the individual components.

Finally, practice showing your work on any multi-step problems, even if you're just studying. Writing out each step you take to solve a problem will help solidify the process in your mind, and you'll be more likely to remember it during the test.

Modality

Modality simply refers to the means or method by which you study. Choosing a study modality that fits your own individual learning style is crucial. No two people learn best in exactly the same way, so it's important to know your strengths and use them to your advantage.

For example, if you learn best by visualization, focus on visualizing a concept in your mind and draw an image or a diagram. Try color-coding your notes, illustrating them, or creating symbols that will trigger your mind to recall a learned concept. If you learn best by hearing or discussing information, find a study partner who learns the same way or read aloud to yourself. Think about how to put the information in your own words. Imagine that you are giving a lecture on the topic and record yourself so you can listen to it later.

For any learning style, flashcards can be helpful. Organize the information so you can take advantage of spare moments to review. Underline key words or phrases. Use different colors for different categories. Mnemonic devices (such as creating a short list in which every item starts with the same letter) can also help with retention. Find what works best for you and use it to store the information in your mind most effectively and easily.

Secret Key #3 – Practice the Right Way

Your success on test day depends not only on how many hours you put into preparing, but also on whether you prepared the right way. It's good to check along the way to see if your studying is paying off. One of the most effective ways to do this is by taking practice tests to evaluate your progress. Practice tests are useful because they show exactly where you need to improve. Every time you take a practice test, pay special attention to these three groups of questions:

- The questions you got wrong
- The questions you had to guess on, even if you guessed right
- The questions you found difficult or slow to work through

This will show you exactly what your weak areas are, and where you need to devote more study time. Ask yourself why each of these questions gave you trouble. Was it because you didn't understand the material? Was it because you didn't remember the vocabulary? Do you need more repetitions on this type of question to build speed and confidence? Dig into those questions and figure out how you can strengthen your weak areas as you go back to review the material.

Additionally, many practice tests have a section explaining the answer choices. It can be tempting to read the explanation and think that you now have a good understanding of the concept. However, an explanation likely only covers part of the question's broader context. Even if the explanation makes perfect sense, **go back and investigate** every concept related to the question until you're positive you have a thorough understanding.

As you go along, keep in mind that the practice test is just that: practice. Memorizing these questions and answers will not be very helpful on the actual test because it is unlikely to have any of the same exact questions. If you only know the right answers to the sample questions, you won't be prepared for the real thing. **Study the concepts** until you understand them fully, and then you'll be able to answer any question that shows up on the test.

It's important to wait on the practice tests until you're ready. If you take a test on your first day of study, you may be overwhelmed by the amount of material covered and how much you need to learn. Work up to it gradually.

On test day, you'll need to be prepared for answering questions, managing your time, and using the test-taking strategies you've learned. It's a lot to balance, like a mental marathon that will have a big impact on your future. Like training for a marathon, you'll need to start slowly and work your way up. When test day arrives, you'll be ready.

Start with the strategies you've read in the first two Secret Keys—plan your course and study in the way that works best for you. If you have time, consider using multiple study resources to get different approaches to the same concepts. It can be helpful to see difficult concepts from more than one angle. Then find a good source for practice tests. Many times, the test website will suggest potential study resources or provide sample tests.

Practice Test Strategy

If you're able to find at least three practice tests, we recommend this strategy:

Untimed and Open-Book Practice

Take the first test with no time constraints and with your notes and study guide handy. Take your time and focus on applying the strategies you've learned.

Timed and Open-Book Practice

Take the second practice test open-book as well, but set a timer and practice pacing yourself to finish in time.

Timed and Closed-Book Practice

Take any other practice tests as if it were test day. Set a timer and put away your study materials. Sit at a table or desk in a quiet room, imagine yourself at the testing center, and answer questions as quickly and accurately as possible.

Keep repeating timed and closed-book tests on a regular basis until you run out of practice tests or it's time for the actual test. Your mind will be ready for the schedule and stress of test day, and you'll be able to focus on recalling the material you've learned.

Secret Key #4 – Pace Yourself

Once you're fully prepared for the material on the test, your biggest challenge on test day will be managing your time. Just knowing that the clock is ticking can make you panic even if you have plenty of time left. Work on pacing yourself so you can build confidence against the time constraints of the exam. Pacing is a difficult skill to master, especially in a high-pressure environment, so **practice is vital**.

Set time expectations for your pace based on how much time is available. For example, if a section has 60 questions and the time limit is 30 minutes, you know you have to average 30 seconds or less per question in order to answer them all. Although 30 seconds is the hard limit, set 25 seconds per question as your goal, so you reserve extra time to spend on harder questions. When you budget extra time for the harder questions, you no longer have any reason to stress when those questions take longer to answer.

Don't let this time expectation distract you from working through the test at a calm, steady pace, but keep it in mind so you don't spend too much time on any one question. Recognize that taking extra time on one question you don't understand may keep you from answering two that you do understand later in the test. If your time limit for a question is up and you're still not sure of the answer, mark it and move on, and come back to it later if the time and the test format allow. If the testing format doesn't allow you to return to earlier questions, just make an educated guess; then put it out of your mind and move on.

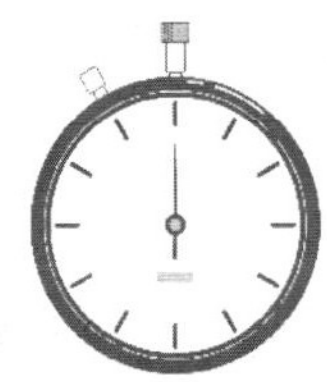

On the easier questions, be careful not to rush. It may seem wise to hurry through them so you have more time for the challenging ones, but it's not worth missing one if you know the concept and just didn't take the time to read the question fully. Work efficiently but make sure you understand the question and have looked at all of the answer choices, since more than one may seem right at first.

Even if you're paying attention to the time, you may find yourself a little behind at some point. You should speed up to get back on track, but do so wisely. Don't panic; just take a few seconds less on each question until you're caught up. Don't guess without thinking, but do look through the answer choices and eliminate any you know are wrong. If you can get down to two choices, it is often worthwhile to guess from those. Once you've chosen an answer, move on and don't dwell on any that you skipped or had to hurry through. If a question was taking too long, chances are it was one of the harder ones, so you weren't as likely to get it right anyway.

On the other hand, if you find yourself getting ahead of schedule, it may be beneficial to slow down a little. The more quickly you work, the more likely you are to make a careless mistake that will affect your score. You've budgeted time for each question, so don't be afraid to spend that time. Practice an efficient but careful pace to get the most out of the time you have.

Secret Key #5 – Have a Plan for Guessing

When you're taking the test, you may find yourself stuck on a question. Some of the answer choices seem better than others, but you don't see the one answer choice that is obviously correct. What do you do?

The scenario described above is very common, yet most test takers have not effectively prepared for it. Developing and practicing a plan for guessing may be one of the single most effective uses of your time as you get ready for the exam.

In developing your plan for guessing, there are three questions to address:

- When should you start the guessing process?
- How should you narrow down the choices?
- Which answer should you choose?

When to Start the Guessing Process

Unless your plan for guessing is to select C every time (which, despite its merits, is not what we recommend), you need to leave yourself enough time to apply your answer elimination strategies. Since you have a limited amount of time for each question, that means that if you're going to give yourself the best shot at guessing correctly, you have to decide quickly whether or not you will guess.

Of course, the best-case scenario is that you don't have to guess at all, so first, see if you can answer the question based on your knowledge of the subject and basic reasoning skills. Focus on the key words in the question and try to jog your memory of related topics. Give yourself a chance to bring the knowledge to mind, but once you realize that you don't have (or you can't access) the knowledge you need to answer the question, it's time to start the guessing process.

It's almost always better to start the guessing process too early than too late. It only takes a few seconds to remember something and answer the question from knowledge. Carefully eliminating wrong answer choices takes longer. Plus, going through the process of eliminating answer choices can actually help jog your memory.

Summary: Start the guessing process as soon as you decide that you can't answer the question based on your knowledge.

How to Narrow Down the Choices

The next chapter in this book (**Test-Taking Strategies**) includes a wide range of strategies for how to approach questions and how to look for answer choices to eliminate. You will definitely want to read those carefully, practice them, and figure out which ones work best for you. Here though, we're going to address a mindset rather than a particular strategy.

Your odds of guessing an answer correctly depend on how many options you are choosing from.

Number of options left	5	4	3	2	1
Odds of guessing correctly	20%	25%	33%	50%	100%

You can see from this chart just how valuable it is to be able to eliminate incorrect answers and make an educated guess, but there are two things that many test takers do that cause them to miss out on the benefits of guessing:

- Accidentally eliminating the correct answer
- Selecting an answer based on an impression

We'll look at the first one here, and the second one in the next section.

To avoid accidentally eliminating the correct answer, we recommend a thought exercise called **the $5 challenge**. In this challenge, you only eliminate an answer choice from contention if you are willing to bet $5 on it being wrong. Why $5? Five dollars is a small but not insignificant amount of money. It's an amount you could afford to lose but wouldn't want to throw away. And while losing $5 once might not hurt too much, doing it twenty times will set you back $100. In the same way, each small decision you make—eliminating a choice here, guessing on a question there—won't by itself impact your score very much, but when you put them all together, they can make a big difference. By holding each answer choice elimination decision to a higher standard, you can reduce the risk of accidentally eliminating the correct answer.

The $5 challenge can also be applied in a positive sense: If you are willing to bet $5 that an answer choice *is* correct, go ahead and mark it as correct.

Summary: Only eliminate an answer choice if you are willing to bet $5 that it is wrong.

Which Answer to Choose

You're taking the test. You've run into a hard question and decided you'll have to guess. You've eliminated all the answer choices you're willing to bet $5 on. Now you have to pick an answer. Why do we even need to talk about this? Why can't you just pick whichever one you feel like when the time comes?

The answer to these questions is that if you don't come into the test with a plan, you'll rely on your impression to select an answer choice, and if you do that, you risk falling into a trap. The test writers know that everyone who takes their test will be guessing on some of the questions, so they intentionally write wrong answer choices to seem plausible. You still have to pick an answer though, and if the wrong answer choices are designed to look right, how can you ever be sure that you're not falling for their trap? The best solution we've found to this dilemma is to take the decision out of your hands entirely. Here is the process we recommend:

Once you've eliminated any choices that you are confident (willing to bet $5) are wrong, select the first remaining choice as your answer.

Whether you choose to select the first remaining choice, the second, or the last, the important thing is that you use some preselected standard. Using this approach guarantees that you will not be enticed into selecting an answer choice that looks right, because you are not basing your decision on how the answer choices look.

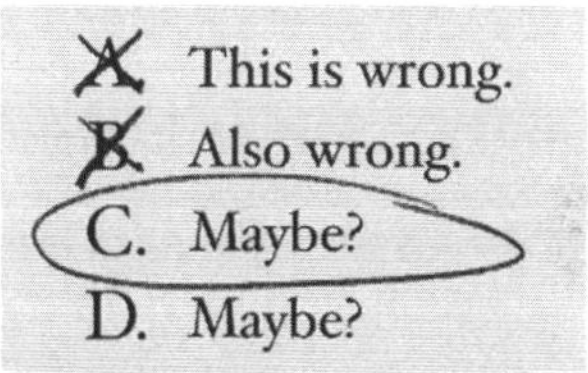

This is not meant to make you question your knowledge. Instead, it is to help you recognize the difference between your knowledge and your impressions. There's a huge difference between thinking an answer is right because of what you know, and thinking an answer is right because it looks or sounds like it should be right.

Summary: To ensure that your selection is appropriately random, make a predetermined selection from among all answer choices you have not eliminated.

Test-Taking Strategies

This section contains a list of test-taking strategies that you may find helpful as you work through the test. By taking what you know and applying logical thought, you can maximize your chances of answering any question correctly!

It is very important to realize that every question is different and every person is different: no single strategy will work on every question, and no single strategy will work for every person. That's why we've included all of them here, so you can try them out and determine which ones work best for different types of questions and which ones work best for you.

Question Strategies

☑ Read Carefully

Read the question and the answer choices carefully. Don't miss the question because you misread the terms. You have plenty of time to read each question thoroughly and make sure you understand what is being asked. Yet a happy medium must be attained, so don't waste too much time. You must read carefully and efficiently.

☑ Contextual Clues

Look for contextual clues. If the question includes a word you are not familiar with, look at the immediate context for some indication of what the word might mean. Contextual clues can often give you all the information you need to decipher the meaning of an unfamiliar word. Even if you can't determine the meaning, you may be able to narrow down the possibilities enough to make a solid guess at the answer to the question.

☑ Prefixes

If you're having trouble with a word in the question or answer choices, try dissecting it. Take advantage of every clue that the word might include. Prefixes can be a huge help. Usually, they allow you to determine a basic meaning. *Pre-* means before, *post-* means after, *pro-* is positive, *de-* is negative. From prefixes, you can get an idea of the general meaning of the word and try to put it into context.

☑ Hedge Words

Watch out for critical hedge words, such as *likely, may, can, often, almost, mostly, usually, generally, rarely*, and *sometimes*. Question writers insert these hedge phrases to cover every possibility. Often an answer choice will be wrong simply because it leaves no room for exception. Be on guard for answer choices that have definitive words such as *exactly* and *always*.

☑ Switchback Words

Stay alert for *switchbacks*. These are the words and phrases frequently used to alert you to shifts in thought. The most common switchback words are *but, although*, and *however*. Others include *nevertheless, on the other hand, even though, while, in spite of, despite*, and *regardless of*. Switchback words are important to catch because they can change the direction of the question or an answer choice.

⊘ Face Value

When in doubt, use common sense. Accept the situation in the problem at face value. Don't read too much into it. These problems will not require you to make wild assumptions. If you have to go beyond creativity and warp time or space in order to have an answer choice fit the question, then you should move on and consider the other answer choices. These are normal problems rooted in reality. The applicable relationship or explanation may not be readily apparent, but it is there for you to figure out. Use your common sense to interpret anything that isn't clear.

Answer Choice Strategies

⊘ Answer Selection

The most thorough way to pick an answer choice is to identify and eliminate wrong answers until only one is left, then confirm it is the correct answer. Sometimes an answer choice may immediately seem right, but be careful. The test writers will usually put more than one reasonable answer choice on each question, so take a second to read all of them and make sure that the other choices are not equally obvious. As long as you have time left, it is better to read every answer choice than to pick the first one that looks right without checking the others.

⊘ Answer Choice Families

An answer choice family consists of two (in rare cases, three) answer choices that are very similar in construction and cannot all be true at the same time. If you see two answer choices that are direct opposites or parallels, one of them is usually the correct answer. For instance, if one answer choice says that quantity x increases and another either says that quantity x decreases (opposite) or says that quantity y increases (parallel), then those answer choices would fall into the same family. An answer choice that doesn't match the construction of the answer choice family is more likely to be incorrect. Most questions will not have answer choice families, but when they do appear, you should be prepared to recognize them.

⊘ Eliminate Answers

Eliminate answer choices as soon as you realize they are wrong, but make sure you consider all possibilities. If you are eliminating answer choices and realize that the last one you are left with is also wrong, don't panic. Start over and consider each choice again. There may be something you missed the first time that you will realize on the second pass.

⊘ Avoid Fact Traps

Don't be distracted by an answer choice that is factually true but doesn't answer the question. You are looking for the choice that answers the question. Stay focused on what the question is asking for so you don't accidentally pick an answer that is true but incorrect. Always go back to the question and make sure the answer choice you've selected actually answers the question and is not merely a true statement.

⊘ Extreme Statements

In general, you should avoid answers that put forth extreme actions as standard practice or proclaim controversial ideas as established fact. An answer choice that states the "process should be used in certain situations, if…" is much more likely to be correct than one that states the "process should be discontinued completely." The first is a calm rational statement and doesn't even make a definitive, uncompromising stance, using a hedge word *if* to provide wiggle room, whereas the second choice is far more extreme.

✓ Benchmark

As you read through the answer choices and you come across one that seems to answer the question well, mentally select that answer choice. This is not your final answer, but it's the one that will help you evaluate the other answer choices. The one that you selected is your benchmark or standard for judging each of the other answer choices. Every other answer choice must be compared to your benchmark. That choice is correct until proven otherwise by another answer choice beating it. If you find a better answer, then that one becomes your new benchmark. Once you've decided that no other choice answers the question as well as your benchmark, you have your final answer.

✓ Predict the Answer

Before you even start looking at the answer choices, it is often best to try to predict the answer. When you come up with the answer on your own, it is easier to avoid distractions and traps because you will know exactly what to look for. The right answer choice is unlikely to be word-for-word what you came up with, but it should be a close match. Even if you are confident that you have the right answer, you should still take the time to read each option before moving on.

General Strategies

✓ Tough Questions

If you are stumped on a problem or it appears too hard or too difficult, don't waste time. Move on! Remember though, if you can quickly check for obviously incorrect answer choices, your chances of guessing correctly are greatly improved. Before you completely give up, at least try to knock out a couple of possible answers. Eliminate what you can and then guess at the remaining answer choices before moving on.

✓ Check Your Work

Since you will probably not know every term listed and the answer to every question, it is important that you get credit for the ones that you do know. Don't miss any questions through careless mistakes. If at all possible, try to take a second to look back over your answer selection and make sure you've selected the correct answer choice and haven't made a costly careless mistake (such as marking an answer choice that you didn't mean to mark). This quick double check should more than pay for itself in caught mistakes for the time it costs.

✓ Pace Yourself

It's easy to be overwhelmed when you're looking at a page full of questions; your mind is confused and full of random thoughts, and the clock is ticking down faster than you would like. Calm down and maintain the pace that you have set for yourself. Especially as you get down to the last few minutes of the test, don't let the small numbers on the clock make you panic. As long as you are on track by monitoring your pace, you are guaranteed to have time for each question.

✓ Don't Rush

It is very easy to make errors when you are in a hurry. Maintaining a fast pace in answering questions is pointless if it makes you miss questions that you would have gotten right otherwise. Test writers like to include distracting information and wrong answers that seem right. Taking a little extra time to avoid careless mistakes can make all the difference in your test score. Find a pace that allows you to be confident in the answers that you select.

⊘ KEEP MOVING

Panicking will not help you pass the test, so do your best to stay calm and keep moving. Taking deep breaths and going through the answer elimination steps you practiced can help to break through a stress barrier and keep your pace.

Final Notes

The combination of a solid foundation of content knowledge and the confidence that comes from practicing your plan for applying that knowledge is the key to maximizing your performance on test day. As your foundation of content knowledge is built up and strengthened, you'll find that the strategies included in this chapter become more and more effective in helping you quickly sift through the distractions and traps of the test to isolate the correct answer.

Now that you're preparing to move forward into the test content chapters of this book, be sure to keep your goal in mind. As you read, think about how you will be able to apply this information on the test. If you've already seen sample questions for the test and you have an idea of the question format and style, try to come up with questions of your own that you can answer based on what you're reading. This will give you valuable practice applying your knowledge in the same ways you can expect to on test day.

Good luck and good studying!

Criminal Behavior

Classical School of Criminology

The classical school of criminology was a philosophy of crime and punishment that originated in the Enlightenment period of the 18th century. It held that humans behaved in a rational manner and that crime was committed out of an individual's free will. It further held that the purpose of punishment was not the enforcement of morality but the deterrence of crime, and that the innocence of the accused criminal should be presumed until proven otherwise. Criminal law should be codified in a written code. Punishments should be proportional to the crime and should prevent the offender and others from committing the crime in the future; however, reformation of the criminal was not the goal. Crime prevention was emphasized. The classical school arose largely from the writings of Cesare Beccaria.

UCR

The Uniform Crime Reports (UCR) is a collection of crime statistics published annually by the FBI. They include tables of statistics on a variety of types of crime, including 8 "index crimes" (including criminal homicide, forcible rape, burglary and arson) as well as 20 other offenses (including fraud, embezzlement, gambling, disorderly conduct, and driving under the influence). The compiled statistics, while informative, include only those crimes reported to the police, and therefore should not be considered a total overview of crime in the US

National Crime Victimization Surveys

The National Crime Victimization Surveys are compiled by the US Census Bureau for the Department of Justice and are based on interviews with individuals in 50,000 households. They attempt to be more statistically complete than the FBI's Uniform Crime Reports, which only list crimes that have been reported to police. However, National Crime Victimization Surveys have been criticized for relying on subjective reports by victims who may underreport certain crimes, such as those for which family members may be criminally culpable, who may have varying perceptions of what constitutes criminal activity, or who may forget significant events and details.

Deviant Behavior

Deviant behavior is behavior judged by society to be unacceptable or outside general behavioral norms. In many cases, deviant behavior is defined as criminal, but not all deviant behavior is illegal nor is all criminal behavior deviant. For instance, dyeing one's hair purple might be considered deviant behavior by some people, but it is not illegal. On the other hand, betting on sporting events is illegal in most jurisdictions, but many people consider it normal and acceptable, even within those jurisdictions. The definition of deviant behavior can change over time and from place to place. For much of the 20th century, homosexual behavior was considered deviant in most of the US and there were laws in many jurisdictions forbidding it, but in recent years it has become increasingly acceptable and the few remaining laws against it are rarely enforced.

Criminal Behavior

In the broadest sense, criminal behavior is behavior that violates criminal law. Thus, criminal behavior is behavior that is explicitly prohibited by the criminal code in a specific jurisdiction and that may be punished by the legal authorities in that jurisdiction. Although criminal behavior generally requires that an act be performed, under some circumstances failure to act can be a crime, and the mere planning of a crime can itself be a crime if it is deemed criminal conspiracy. In most cases, criminal intent -- the conscious intent to commit a legally prohibited act -- is necessary for an act to be considered criminal. Inadvertent criminal behavior is generally not punishable, except where the inadvertent act is performed during the commission of a different criminal act or while acting recklessly. Criminal behavior by an individual deemed mentally incapable of recognizing the criminal nature of the act also fails to be considered as a crime.

Mens Rea

Mens rea, a Latin expression meaning "guilty mind," is the conscious awareness on the part of an individual that they are committing an illegal act and, in most cases, is necessary before the act can be considered criminal. In order to prove that mens rea exists, the law must prove that an act was committed:

- Purposefully -- with conscious intent to produce an illegal result;
- Knowingly -- with conscious awareness that the act will lead to the illegal result;
- Recklessly -- with awareness that the act could possibly produce the illegal result even though that result was not the specific intent of the act; or
- Negligently -- without awareness that the act could produce the illegal result, but in circumstances where a reasonable person could have anticipated the result.

If one or more of these mental states is shown to have been present, then mens rea is proven. However, different crimes require different levels of mens rea and some crimes, such as murder, require specific intent.

Entrapment and Intent

Entrapment occurs in a situation where authorities are found to have encouraged an individual to perform a criminal act in which they would not otherwise have engaged. For instance, a so-called sting operation in which police sell narcotics or child pornography to an individual could be considered entrapment if it can be shown that the individual was not predisposed to make the purchase before the illegal materials were offered. Entrapment can be considered an inducement to perform an illegal act. Most criminal acts require that some degree of intent be present, and entrapment allows the defense to show lack of intent on the part of a criminal defendant. In a 1992 Supreme Court decision, Justice Byron White declared that authorities may not "originate a criminal design, implant in an innocent person's mind the disposition to commit a criminal act, and then induce commission of the crime so that the government may prosecute."

Actus Reus

Actus reus, a Latin term meaning "guilty act," is the physical action or external process involved in the commission of a crime. In order to prove that a crime has been committed, the prosecution generally must demonstrate both the actus reus, or physical act, and the mens rea, or mental state, showing deliberate intent or negligence. The actus reus usually involves some sort of bodily movement, though in a few cases it can be defined as the failure to perform an act (where that failure leads to an illegal result). The actus reus can also be the possession of illicit materials, even though possession itself is not normally characterized as an act and does not involve bodily movement.

Misprision of Felony

In the broadest sense, misprision means not performing a public duty. In criminal law, however, it usually refers to hiding a crime. Misprision of felony occurs when someone is aware that someone else has committed a felony offense, but does not report this information to the proper authorities. Misprision of felony can be a crime in itself and does not involve any participation in or abetting of the crime other than awareness of information that could be used to apprehend the perpetrators, even if that information was accidentally overheard. Failing to prevent a felony may also be considered misprision, as can lying to a police officer investigating a felony case. The concept of misprision of felony comes from English common law and is rarely invoked in the United States, following an 1822 Supreme Court decision that found punishment for failing to report a crime overly harsh.

VICARIOUS LIABILITY

Vicarious liability is a type of secondary liability, under which one person can be held responsible for the acts of another. The most common use of this concept, sometimes referred to by the Latin term respondeat superior, is to hold an employer responsible for illegal acts committed by an employee in their normal course of duties. For example, the owner of a store can be held responsible when a clerk employed by the store sells alcoholic beverages to a minor. Another type of vicarious liability is the responsibility of an automobile owner for damage caused by someone who has borrowed that automobile.

MALICE AFORETHOUGHT

The legal expression malice aforethought refers to criminal intent or mens rea, the knowledge on the part of a person committing a criminal act that the act is in fact criminal. Because proving that a criminal act has been committed usually requires proving intent, the establishment of malice aforethought is an important element of proving that a crime has been committed. These words are generally part of the description of the crime itself and are commonly used in charging a criminal defendant, especially when death or physical harm to a victim is involved.

DURESS AND COERCION

In order for a crime to have taken place, intent must be present. If a person commits a crime against their own intentions because they have been forced to against their will -- by threats to their well being, for instance, or threats to the well being of others -- then they are said to have acted under duress. An individual cannot be held legally responsible for acts performed under duress. The act of forcing someone to commit a crime under duress is called coercion and is itself a crime. Both the actus reus and mens reus can be present in the commission of the crime, with the accused having performed the criminal act in full awareness of its criminal nature, but the accused can be declared innocent or given a lesser sentence because coercion was present.

JUSTIFICATION

Justification can be used as a defense in criminal prosecutions. It suggests that the accused was justified in performing what otherwise would be a criminal act. For instance, if a murder is committed in self-defense, it can be ruled justifiable homicide. This is not an excuse because the homicide was still committed and the accused was fully aware of his or her actions. On the other hand, if the accused is found to be mentally incapable of comprehending the nature of the criminal act -- because of insanity, immaturity, or other exculpating factor -- the act can be considered excusable. Thus, an excusable act occurs when the accused is not capable of understanding the full significance of the actions performed.

MALICE AFORETHOUGHT

The legal expression malice aforethought refers to criminal intent or mens rea, the knowledge on the part of a person committing a criminal act that the act is in fact criminal. Because proving that a criminal act has been committed usually requires proving intent, the establishment of malice aforethought is an important element of proving that a crime has been committed. These words are generally part of the description of the crime itself and are commonly used in charging a criminal defendant, especially when death or physical harm to a victim is involved.

Insanity Defense

The insanity defense, which attempts to prove that a defendant is not guilty by reason of insanity, is based on the concept that a crime cannot be committed without mens rea -- that is, an awareness that the act committed is, in fact, wrong. The insanity defense assumes that a person suffering from certain forms of mental illness cannot be aware of the criminal nature of the act being performed. The insanity defense, which derives from the legal principles established by the M'Naghten Rule, the Durham Rule and other precedents for determining the mental inability of a person to judge their own actions, is controversial. Persons found not responsible for a crime by reason of insanity are often confined to mental hospitals instead of prisons, and the amount of time which they are confined is in some cases longer than they would have been confined to prison without the insanity defense.

Mistake of Fact

Mistake of fact is a defense used in criminal cases that attempts to show that the criminal action resulted from some kind of misunderstanding. For instance, the purchase of stolen goods is usually regarded as a criminal act, unless the buyer can prove that the purchase was made without knowledge that the goods were stolen. Similarly, if the defendant has taken someone else's properly while mistakenly believing that the property is his or her own, then it is not necessarily a crime. The mistake of fact must be both honest and reasonable. It cannot be the result of criminal negligence, and for some crimes a condition of strict liability exists. For instance, mistake of fact is not necessarily an excuse for selling alcohol or tobacco to a minor and is generally not a valid excuse in cases of statutory rape, even if the defendant claims not to have been aware of the sex partner's age.

Mistake of Law

Mistake of law is a defense used in criminal cases that attempts to prove that the criminal action resulted from a misunderstanding of the law itself. If successful, it demonstrates that the defendant does not have the necessary mens rea, or "guilty mind," because he/she was not in fact aware that the act he/she was performing was illegal. However, this defense is rarely successful and in most cases the maxim "Ignorance of the law is no excuse" prevails. The few instances in which this defense can be successful include cases where the law was not made reasonably available to the public, or in which the defendant had been misinformed about the law by appropriate authorities. Misinformation provided by a lawyer is not generally considered exculpatory.

Constitutional Law

Constitutional law is that body of laws codified in the United States Constitution and the constitutions of the individual states. It specifies how the government can exercise its power and what the limits of that power are. Other forms of law, such as statutory law and administrative law, may address areas that are not covered by constitutional law, but must still conform to constitutional law. Constitutional law also refers to the interpretations of the constitutions by the United States Supreme Court and the supreme courts of the states. Constitutional law can be changed through amendments to the constitutions. Constitutional law is the supreme law of the land in that it supersedes any other forms of law with which it may come into conflict. Constitutional law drawn from the US Constitution also supersedes law drawn from the state constitutions.

Statutory Law and Case Law

Statutory law is that body of laws, or statutes, enacted by the legislature at the federal, state or local level. Statutory law generally concerns itself with matters not specifically covered by constitutional law, but it must not violate constitutional law (either from the US Constitution or the relevant state constitution) for the jurisdictions in which the laws are enacted. Statutory law specifies, in detail, precisely which acts are treated by authorities as illegal and prescribes punishments for them. Statutory law is different from common law in that it is enacted through formal legislative processes and codified in written form. In some cases, statutory law is also based on the rules and regulations of administrative law. The interpretations of these statutes in the courts become case law, a set of legal precedents that is then used to guide judges in their application of the statutes.

COMMON LAW

Common law is law based on the customs of society as interpreted by judges. Common law is not based in written law or statutes, but in the decisions of the courts. The concept of common law originated in England and was brought to America by British colonists. It is distinguished from civil law, which originated in Roman society. Civil law is collected in written form, usually as enacted by a legislature. Historically, the strength of common law has been its flexibility while the strength of civil law is its clarity and certainty. Common law is also distinguished from case law, which also comes from court decisions but is based in statutes rather than customs.

ADMINISTRATIVE LAW

Administrative law, also known as regulatory law, consists of the rules and regulations created by, and sometimes governing, the actions of government agencies, e.g., the Food and Drug Administration (FDA), the Federal Trade Commission (FTC), Federal Communications Commission (FCC), the Drug Enforcement Administration (DEA), and others. According to the Administrative Procedure Act of 1946, agencies may create rules and make judicial decisions concerning the areas that they are charged with overseeing in much the same way that the federal government does. Administrative law has the full force of the legal system behind it in the United States, but is also subject to the same constitutional limitations to which other types of law are subject.

COMPARATIVE CRIMINOLOGY

Comparative criminology is the study of crime and patterns of crime across multiple cultures. It is an attempt to expand criminal theory beyond western culture, where it has largely been restricted until recently. It makes use of a number of other areas of study, including anthropology and sociology. Comparative criminology is considered of increased importance following the September 11 attacks, which have their roots in culture clash and ethnocentrism. Those behaviors considered criminal can vary considerably between cultures -- for instance, between western cultures and Middle Eastern cultures -- and understanding the differences can not only improve our understanding of those cultures, but reduce cross-cultural friction.

OMNIBUS CRIME CONTROL AND SAFE STREETS ACT OF 1968

The Omnibus Crime Control and Safe Streets Act was passed by Congress in 1968. It established the Law Enforcement Assistance Administration (LEAA), which funded criminal justice research. It also attempted to overrule Supreme Court decisions concerning requirements that suspects be informed of their rights, and it allowed wiretapping without a warrant. The act was highly controversial at the time and was believed by many to be nothing more than a political gesture in reaction to public fears that crime was out of control. The Act's opponents felt that it was reducing the due process rights of accused criminals and risked establishing a police state.

USA PATRIOT ACT

The USA Patriot Act was passed by Congress in the wake of, and in response to, the September 11, 2001, attacks on the World Trade Center buildings and the Pentagon. The Act's name is an acronym for Uniting and Strengthening America by Providing Appropriate Tools Required to Intercept and Obstruct Terrorism. Its purpose is to protect the United States against future terrorist acts, and it expands the ability of authorities to enforce the law in ways often regarded as violations of due process. For instance, it allows the indefinite imprisonment of individuals suspected of involvement in terrorism without being charged and the wiretapping of phone lines without warrant.

LAW AND ORDER

The term "law and order" was commonly used in the 1960s and '70s to represent a philosophy which held that government had become overly permissive with lawbreakers and granted too many rights to those suspected of criminal behavior. It was a reaction to perceived lawlessness in the 1960s and to Supreme Court rulings such as Miranda v. Arizona, in which it was determined that confessions could become inadmissible in court if the suspect was not advised that he or she had a right to remain silent and consult an attorney. "Law and order" was also a response to increasingly permissive behavior among younger people in regard to sex and drugs. It was used on several occasions as a campaign phrase by politicians.

BIOLOGICAL THEORIES OF CRIME CAUSATION

The biological school of crime causation is a set of theories that attempt to explain criminal behavior in anthropological and genetic terms. They are based on the concept of biological determinism, which holds that behavior has its roots in the body. These include theories that criminal behavior is inherited within families, is caused by aberrant chromosomes, or is influenced by body type. These theories were common in the late 19th and early 20th centuries, but came to be disregarded in the mid- 20th century because of fears that they reinforced racist stereotypes and could be used to justify the idea that some ethnic groups are genetically inferior or prone to violence. Recent studies into the human genome have revived interest in these theories, but they remain controversial.

CESARE LOMBROSO

Cesare Lombroso (1835-1909) is considered the father of modern criminology and the founder of criminal anthropology. He believed that a criminal nature was inborn. He attempted to demonstrate that certain physical features, such as large ears, a sloping forehead and malformed teeth were associated with criminals and could be used to identify criminals independently of behavior. His theories were strongly influenced by the work of evolutionary biologist Charles Darwin, and he felt that criminals were a throwback to an earlier stage of evolution. Although Lombroso's work has few modern supporters and has been superseded by modern theories of anthropology, he was an important early proponent of the biological school of crime causation.

ANOMIE THEORY

Anomie theory comes from the work of 19th century French sociologist Émile Durkheim, who proposed that a lack of social standards and societal norms -- a condition known as normlessness -- could produce a breakdown in moral behavior and an increase in social disorder. He believed that such conditions could lead to selfish, even criminal, behavior as well as suicide. Durkheim held that normlessness was common in times of economic change and under conditions where the goals valued by society become difficult for many members of that society to achieve. Sociologist Robert K. Merton used anomie theory as the basis for his strain theory of criminal behavior.

STRAIN THEORY BY ROBERT K. MERTON

In the 1930s, American sociologist Robert K. Merton developed a theory of crime causation based on Émile Durkheim's anomie theory. He proposed that criminal behavior results from the strain between socially-approved aspirations and the means available for achieving them, which were often inadequate; thus, Merton's ideas on crime causation are known as strain theory. Merton believed that there were several adaptations, or modes, which people made to resolve this strain:

- Conformity -- Conforming to the rules of society even though this may mean not achieving goals. This, according to Merton, is the most common mode
- Innovation -- Attempting to find new, but often socially disapproved, ways of achieving individual goals
- Rejection -- Rejecting society's goals and the means for achieving them, even to the point of overthrowing the system
- Retreatism -- Dropping out of society and giving up all hopes of achieving goals
- Ritualism -- Rejecting society's goals, but mindlessly following its rules for achieving them

General Strain Theory by Robert Agnew

General strain theory represents a modification and expansion of the work of sociologist Robert K. Merton, who proposed that criminal behavior represented an adaptation to the strain between society's goals and its prescribed means for achieving them. The general strain theories of sociologist Robert Agnew emphasize the role of negative emotions created by this strain, such as anger, depression and anxiety. He identified three types of strain that he believed led to the emotions that produced deviant social behavior:

- Failure to achieve positively valued goals -- This can result not just from the gap between society's rules and its goals, but from circumstances in an individual's life.
- Removal of positively-valued stimuli -- These stimuli can include positive relationships or a good job. They can be removed by a death, a divorce, a move to a new physical location or acquiring a new job.
- Confrontation with negative stimuli -- These negative stimuli can include unhealthy relationships, negative peer pressure, and child abuse.

Differential Opportunity Theory of Crime Causation

Differential opportunity theory was proposed by sociologists Richard Cloward and Lloyd Ohlin in their 1960 book Delinquency and Opportunity: A Theory of Delinquent Gangs. They suggested that criminal behavior is opportunistic, and that people in different walks of life commit different kinds of crime because they have access to those crimes. Criminal opportunities are determined by the social structure of a community. People who live in an economically-disadvantaged area may have access to one form of crime (those committed by street gangs, for instance), while high income workers have access to another kind (embezzling and other so-called white collar crimes). Communities with more criminal activity are those where there are more opportunities for crime.

Differential Association Theory of Crime Causation

Differential association theory, developed by sociologist and criminologist Edwin Sutherland, holds that criminal behavior is a form of conformity and is learned by associating with criminals in the context of intimate social groups. People shape their lives according to a set of definitions learned from experience, and individuals will choose a path in life that conforms to the lifestyle, including criminal lifestyles, for which they have the most definitions. Social associations with criminals, especially those who have a high status within the community, increase the number of criminal definitions and will not only lead an individual to adopt a criminal lifestyle, but will impart the skills and knowledge necessary for that lifestyle.

DIFFERENTIAL REINFORCEMENT THEORY OF CRIME CAUSATION

Differential reinforcement theory is a variation on differential association theory that adds the concept of instrumental conditioning (also known as operant conditioning), the modification of behavior based on the consequences of that behavior. Behavior that is reinforced through positive consequences is favored over behavior that produces negative consequences. Differential association theory posits that criminal behavior is learned from associating socially with criminals, but differential reinforcement suggests that this is because criminal behavior is given positive social reinforcement through these associations. Criminal behavior is explained by this theory through four key concepts:

- Differential association (where association with criminals encourages criminal behavior)
- Differential reinforcement of criminal and non-criminal behaviors
- Imitation of observed criminal behaviors inspired by the success of those behaviors
- Definitions of criminal behavior internalized by the individual

SOCIAL CONTROL THEORY OF CRIME CAUSATION

Social control theory, as developed by sociologist Travis Hirschi in his 1969 book Causes of Delinquency, posits that criminal behavior results not so much from social influences on the individual leading toward criminal behavior as from the lack of social influences inhibiting that behavior. Hirschi felt that the most important factor in resisting criminal behavior is the social bond that connects an individual to non-criminal society. In this theory there are four types of social bond:

- Attachment to non-criminal society, including relatives, friends and teachers
- Commitment to a non-criminal way of life and to non-criminal activities
- Involvement in non-criminal activity
- Beliefs in moral standards of living

Hirschi believed that those who felt they had a stake in conforming to the standards of non-criminal society would more likely choose a non-criminal lifestyle.

HOMICIDE

Homicide is the act of killing a human being. It is not synonymous with murder, which is the killing of another human being with malicious intent. Under some circumstances homicide is considered justifiable -- for instance, when a soldier kills an enemy soldier in a war or when someone is killed in self- defense. A police officer may justifiably kill a person to prevent them from committing certain felony crimes. Homicide is considered excusable if it is committed accidentally in the course of a lawful act and without recklessness or negligence. To be considered murder, a homicide requires some degree of mens rea, or guilty intent, though homicides committed through negligence or reckless behavior can in many instances be considered murder.

MURDER

Murder is an act of homicide (the killing of a human being) committed with criminal intent. Depending on the circumstances under which it is committed, murder can be treated under the law with varying degrees of seriousness. The most serious form of murder is first-degree murder, which is generally defined as a deliberate, premeditated act of homicide. In many jurisdictions, first-degree murder is a capital crime and is punishable by death. In some states, certain forms of murder, such as murder by poison or the murder of a police officer, are automatically considered first-degree murder. Second degree murder is defined as a murder that does not meet the standards of premeditation for first-degree murder, does not fall into the categories of murder defined by law as first-degree murder, or that is committed during a felonious act. Some states, in reaction to a 1972 Supreme Court ruling that imposed new restrictions on the application of the death penalty, have created additional degrees of murder.

Felony-Murder Doctrine

The felony-murder doctrine, which derives from common law and has been incorporated into statutory law in many states, holds that any death that occurs during the commission of a felony can be treated as first-degree murder and that all participants in the felony can be charged with murder, even if the death was accidental. This doctrine is an exception to the general rule that first-degree murder must be deliberate and premeditated. For instance, if someone dies as a result of arson or is hit and killed by the getaway car after a bank robbery, the participants in that arson or the bank robbery can be tried for first-degree murder, though minor participants in the crime may be excluded.

Mass Murderer, Spree Killer, and Serial Killer

A mass murderer is someone who commits multiple murders on a single occasion, usually over the course of a few hours or days, and at a single location. Mass murderers are often mentally disturbed and driven by rage or despair. Examples include Charles Whitman, who shot and killed 14 people and wounded 32 others from the tower atop the administration building at the University of Texas in Austin in 1966. A spree killer commits multiple murders over the course of days or weeks but at multiple locations. Examples include Charles Starkweather and his girlfriend Caril Ann Fugate, who murdered 11 people in a killing spree across Nebraska and Wyoming in 1958. A serial killer is a murderer who kills three or more victims over a period of months or years. Serial killers are generally white males in their 20s or 30s, of above average intelligence, and plan their murders methodically. An example would be Ted Bundy, who raped and murdered at least 26 women, and possibly more than 100, between 1973 and 1978.

The four types of serial killer defined by Holmes are:

1. The Visionary, a psychotic killer who believes he or she is driven to commit murder by imaginary entities such as the devil or a demon (or even God)
2. The Power-Oriented Killer, who wants to dominate or control his or her victims
3. The Mission-Oriented Killer, who commits murder to rid the world of a certain type of victim that the killer deems undesirable
4. The Hedonistic Killer, who commits murder for the sheer, often sexual, thrill

Manslaughter

Manslaughter is a form of homicide that, while neither justifiable nor excusable, nonetheless does not involve criminal intent. It is generally broken down into two categories:

- Voluntary manslaughter, in which homicide is committed intentionally but without malice, e.g., in the heat of passion. An example would be a murder committed during a heated argument.
- Involuntary manslaughter, in which homicide occurs accidentally but negligently or in the course of a criminal act. Examples would include killing someone while driving drunk.

The interpretation of manslaughter can vary from jurisdiction to jurisdiction and even from judge to judge. For instance, a homicide that occurs accidentally during a felony may be ruled involuntary manslaughter or, under the felony-murder doctrine, first-degree murder. Furthermore, crimes of passion may be ruled either voluntary manslaughter or second-degree murder, depending on the circumstances and the judgment of the court.

Assault and battery

Assault is a threat of physical harm that may or may not include bodily contact, but no violence or harm to the victim. The infliction of nonfatal physical injury is called battery. Types of assault include:

- Simple assault is assault that threatens someone, but with no actual harm occurring.
- Aggravated assault is assault with intent to cause harm, as opposed to assault intended to frighten or intimidate.
- Assault and battery is assault leading to actual physical harm or violence.
- Menacing is assault involving simple physical contact with a victim.
- Mayhem is assault that disfigures someone or removes a body part.
- Jostling is assault by pushing or shoving the victim. In some jurisdictions, picking someone's pocket can be considered jostling.

Arson

Arson is setting a fire with criminal intent. The fire can be intended to destroy property, such as a dwelling or commercial building, or a natural area, such as woodlands. The property may belong to the arsonist (who may be setting the fire to hide evidence of a crime or for insurance purposes), or it may belong to someone else. Arson is always a felony. In some jurisdictions there are degrees of arson established by statute:

- First-degree arson is setting fire to occupied premises.
- Second-degree arson is setting fire to unoccupied premises not owned by the arsonist.
- Third-degree arson is setting fire to unoccupied premises owned by the arsonist.

Because arson requires malicious intent, it is necessary for prosecutors to establish a motive. Motives for arson can vary and include revenge, insurance fraud, vandalism, hiding criminal evidence, or excitement.

Burglary

Burglary is entering or attempting to enter a building with the intention of committing a crime (usually, but not always, theft). The term breaking and entering is used for some types of burglary, but breaking into a building is not always necessary for an act to be considered burglary. Attempted entry can also constitute burglary as can staying in a building after authorized hours for criminal purposes. Some jurisdictions recognize varying degrees of burglary:

- First-degree burglary is defined as burglary of a dwelling while armed that includes physical injury to someone.
- Second-degree burglary is defined as burglary of a dwelling while armed or with physical injury to someone, but not both.
- Third-degree burglary is defined as burglary by an unarmed burglar with no resulting physical injury.

Larceny, Shoplifting and Pickpocketing

Larceny is taking property owned by another person, without the owner's consent, with the intent of permanently depriving them of that property. This must be personal property, and not real estate, for the theft to be considered larceny. Shoplifting is taking goods from a merchant without their permission. This can include fraudulently paying the wrong price -- by switching price tags, for example. It can also include taking property other than merchandise, such as a shopping cart.

Pickpocketing is taking property directly from a person's clothing, or from their purse, backpack, briefcase, or other object carried on their person.

DOMESTIC VIOLENCE

Domestic violence refers to physically violent actions within a family or close relationship. It can include various forms of abuse, including physical abuse (or battery) and psychological abuse, including harassment. It can also include rape (including marital rape and date rape), aggravated assault, child molestation, and even murder. Domestic violence can occur between spouses, between parents and children, between siblings, or between unrelated individuals in the same household. Men can perpetrate violence on women, and women can perpetrate violence on men. Violence against children has been defined to include, in some cases, the use of drugs during pregnancy.

HATE CRIME

A hate crime is a crime committed out of bias against a person's membership in some larger group, based on ethnicity, sexual orientation, religion, political affiliation, disability, nationality, sex, age, and so forth. Hate crimes are generally acts such as assault, murder, and harassment that would be considered criminal even if bias were not involved, though some hate crimes, such as burning a cross on a black family's lawn or painting a swastika on a synagogue, are specific to the prejudice motivating the crime. There is debate as to whether hate crimes should be punished more harshly than similar crimes not motivated by bias, with one side arguing that hate crimes are intended not only to harm the victim but to threaten or intimidate the larger group to which they belong, and the other side arguing that treating hate crimes separately violates the principle of equal protection under the law.

WHITE COLLAR CRIME

White collar crimes are nonviolent crimes committed by employees within the course of their jobs. According to criminologist Edwin Sutherland, these crimes are usually perpetrated by individuals with high socioeconomic status and are typically committed for economic gain. White collar crimes often, but not always, involve the violation of a trusted position within a company. A wide variety of criminal acts can be considered white collar crimes, including embezzlement, consumer fraud, false advertising, insider stock trading, monopolistic business practices, insurance fraud, restraint of trade, patent and copyright infringement, bribery (both making bribes and accepting them), and illegal campaign practices.

ORGANIZED CRIME

Organized crime is crime systematically organized as a form of business enterprise, with that enterprise engaging in profit-making operations that are often unlawful. These include the promotion of gambling, trafficking and manufacture of illegal drugs, loan sharking, and prostitution. Generally the purpose of organized crime is the same as that of legitimate business: financial profit. Organized crime can be committed on a national or even international level and the individuals involved tend to see crime as a career in which they will remain engaged for much of their lives. Crime organizations generally have a hierarchical structure, with bosses at the highest level, lieutenants at the middle level and ordinary criminals at the lowest level. Crime organizations can work together cooperatively. Organized crime is often seen by those at the lower socioeconomic levels as a means of gaining respect and economic success.

TERRORISM

Terrorism is politically- motivated violence. It is invariably considered criminal activity. It can include such crimes as murder, assault and battery, destruction of property, airplane hijacking and kidnapping, as long as those crimes are performed with the intent of altering the political process in some way. It is rarely a direct attack on whatever political mechanism is meant to be affected, but on innocent victims with the intent of politically and ideologically influencing others. Terrorism has been around for centuries if not millennia. The most famous terrorist act of recent years was almost certainly the September 11, 2001, attacks in New York and Virginia.

Status Offense

A status offense is an act that is considered a crime only if it is performed by a juvenile. They include running away from home, unexcused absences from school, violating curfew, incorrigible behavior, or underage consumption of alcohol and tobacco. Status offenses are usually tried in juvenile court and, because they would not be criminal behavior if committed by an adult, are not classified as delinquency. The concept of the status offense derives from the philosophy of parens patriae, which says that the state can serve a parental role when parents fail to govern the unruly behavior of a child.

Embezzlement, Fraud, Forgery, and Counterfeiting

Embezzlement is the theft of money by an employee or employees who have been entrusted with the care of that money. Fraud is the taking of money or property or the perpetration of damage to an individual or group of individuals through the false representation of facts or some form of criminal deception. Forgery is fraud committed through intentional alteration of documents or legal instruments. Counterfeiting is the forging of currency or of documents representing an obligation on the part of an organization or government and the representation of these counterfeit objects as real.

Disorderly Conduct, Disturbing the Peace, Breach of the Peace, Drunkenness, and Public Intoxication

Disorderly conduct is public behavior that is unruly or found to be disturbing to others, or that violates the public sense of decency. Disturbing the peace is similar to disorderly conduct, but specifically concerns disruptions to the peace and quiet of a community or public area. Breach of the peace is used to describe serious disruptions of public order including not just disorderly conduct but resisting arrest, trespassing, and performing violent actions that damage property. Drunkenness is extreme intoxication, often to the point of physical or mental helplessness. Public intoxication is disorderly conduct committed while under the influence of an intoxicating substance, usually alcohol.

Misdemeanor and Felony

Not all criminal offenses are regarded as carrying the same level of seriousness. Those offenses known as felonies are judged to be the most harmful and are given the harshest punishment. In some instances, they are even punishable by death. Crimes considered felonies typically include murder, rape, grand theft, sale of illegal drugs, and aggravated assault. In some jurisdictions, felonies themselves are ranked by degree of seriousness, with lower-degree felonies carrying lesser sentences. Prison sentences for felonies are typically one year or longer and take place in federal or state penitentiaries. Misdemeanors are relatively minor offenses, usually punishable either by fine or by a sentence of less than a year in a local jail. Crimes considered to be misdemeanors vary between jurisdictions, but can include trespassing, prostitution, petty theft, and public drunkenness.

Juvenile Delinquency

Legally, the term delinquency refers to behavior performed by someone too young to be considered an adult that would be considered criminal behavior if performed by an adult. A juvenile delinquent is someone who engages in such behavior. Procedures for dealing with juvenile delinquents are generally different from those used to deal with adult criminals. The juvenile court system was established in the first half of the 20th century to handle delinquency in a manner that protected both society and the delinquents themselves. The age at which an offender is considered an adult varies from state to state, but ranges from 16 to 18.

IMPORTANT TERMS

- Abettor - An abettor is a person who abets, or assists, in the commission of a crime, but is not directly involved in the criminal act itself. For instance, an abettor may assist the principals in planning the crime or may aid the getaway.
- Accessory after the fact - An accessory after the fact is someone who is aware that the principals have committed a crime and assists them after a crime is committed -- for instance, by sheltering them or otherwise helping them to escape the law.
- Accessory before the fact - An accessory before the fact is an abettor who helps plan or provide support for a crime but isn't present when it is committed.
- Principal - A principal is a person who performs a criminal action.

Criminal Justice System

US Constitution

The Constitution of the United States, adopted in 1787 and written mainly by James Madison, is the cornerstone of all American law. It represents the supreme law of the United States of America and supersedes all laws drafted subsequently by the federal government and the individual states, which must conform to it. The Constitution is interpreted by the courts, most importantly the United States Supreme Court, which has the last word on constitutional issues. The Constitution may be amended by a two-thirds vote of both houses of Congress and the ratification of three-fourths of the states. Several amendments to the Constitution, especially the first ten amendments (or Bill of Rights), spell out rights of due process that must be observed throughout the criminal justice system.

President's Commission on Law Enforcement and Administration of Justice

The President's Commission on Law Enforcement and Administration of Justice was established on July 25, 1965, as part of President Lyndon Baines Johnson's "war on crime." It was a response to perceived increases in lawlessness during the 1960s, including the assassination of President John F. Kennedy in November of 1963. The task given the Commission was to examine the role of the Federal government in crime prevention. In 1967, the Commission produced a report entitled The Challenge of Crime in a Free Society, which made a series of recommendations for changes that the commissioners believed were needed in the American criminal justice system. These recommendations were highly influential and had a profound effect on criminal justice in the United States.

Substantive Criminal Law and Procedural Criminal Law

Substantive Criminal Law is that body of law that defines which acts are considered criminal by the government and that prescribes punishments for those acts. These laws are created by legislators on the national, state and local levels, and are interpreted by judges during criminal proceedings. Procedural Criminal Law concerns those procedures that are used to enforce the law and to determine the legal culpability of a defendant in a criminal case. In many cases, these laws protect the rights of the accused and are based on constitutional freedoms granted at both the state and national level. Although these laws can also be created in the legislature, they are frequently defined by the US Supreme Court and the supreme courts of the various states. Procedural Criminal Law is based in the Due Process Model of criminal justice.

Criminal Law and Civil Law

Criminal law is that body of laws which concerns itself with acts that threaten society as a whole. These are acts such as murder, theft, and rape that threaten the general safety and well-being of the public. Civil law is concerned with grievances between entities such as individuals and corporations. Civil law concerns itself with contract violations, real estate disputes, and situations in which an individual may feel that they have been deprived of rights they believe to be theirs. Many events can be treated under both civil and criminal law, though generally the standards of proof and the requirements of intent are more stringent under criminal law. Civil law disputes are generally resolved through lawsuits, rather than criminal prosecution, and are punished by compensation to the injured party rather than by jail sentence or fine.

Criminal Justice Areas of Study

The study of criminal justice actually consists of four different areas of study. They are:

- Criminology -- The study of crime itself, along with its causes, its prevention and the rehabilitation of criminals.
- Criminal law -- The branch of law that deals with crime and defines what constitutes a criminal act.
- Criminal procedure -- The procedures applied by the police and the courts to find an accused suspect guilty or innocent of a crime.
- Constitutional law -- The branch of law that deals with the United States Constitution, which limits the ability of government to pass laws and defines the rights of those accused under the legal system.

War on Drugs

The term "war on drugs" is used to describe a series of government actions that began in the late 1960s in response to perceived increases in the use of illicit drugs in several different layers of American society. The term was coined by President Richard M. Nixon. The war on drugs includes laws aimed at preventing the flow of illegal drugs into the United States and the manufacture and distribution of drugs within its borders. The war on drugs has been extremely expensive, and some people question whether it has been worth the effort in terms of benefits to society when it has also filled prisons with people who have committed no crimes other than drug possession. Some have suggested that the way to end the violence and crime created by the drug industry is to legalize the drugs, though this is a very controversial proposed solution and is unlikely to be feasible politically.

Victimology

Victimology studies the role of the victim in crime. One of its most interesting revelations is that some people are more likely to become crime victims than others. Certain behaviors, lifestyles, geographic regions, and professions lend themselves more to becoming a victim. For instance, studies have shown that inner city youths are much more likely than the ordinary person to become crime victims because of the people with whom they associate and the environment in which they live. By the same token, elderly white females are relatively unlikely to become crime victims.

Characteristics of the Criminal Justice System

The four major characteristics of the criminal justice system are:

1. Discretion - The ability of police, prosecutors, judges and others in the criminal justice system to use their judgment on such issues as whether to prosecute, what sentence to impose, what charges will be filed, etc.
2. Resource dependence -- The dependence of law enforcement organizations on resources provided from outside the organization, such as funding.
3. Sequential tasks -- The sequence of ordered steps necessary to find a suspect guilty or innocent of a crime.
4. Filtering -- The decision process that can lead to the suspect being removed from the criminal justice system at any stage up to the correctional stage.

Criminal Justice System as a Filtering Process

There are many stages in the criminal justice system leading up to conviction or exoneration. At any stage, it may be decided that the person believed to have committed the crime should not go to trial. In fact, only a small percentage of suspects actually reach the point of being convicted for a crime. The police may decide that evidence is insufficient for arrest, the prosecutor may decide that there is insufficient evidence to prosecute, or that some alternative other than the courts would be appropriate for the case. The defendant may also be found not guilty in a trial. Either way, the suspect can be filtered out at multiple stages of the process.

Crime Control Model and the Due Process Model

In the Crime Control Model of criminal justice, the most important function of the criminal justice system is to deter crime. To that end, the processing of accused criminals should be swift and efficient, and police should not be hampered by legal technicalities. The rights of the victims are considered more important than the rights of the defendants. The Due Process Model emphasizes constitutional protections for the accused, as well as the concept that the defendant in a court case is innocent until proven guilty. The rights of the defendant are considered paramount in this model because they protect the wrongfully accused from unjust punishment. Generally speaking, the Crime Control Model is espoused by political conservatives while the Due Process Model is espoused by political liberals. The two models were originally described by Herbert Packer in his 1968 book The Limits of the Criminal Sanction.

Bill of Rights

The Bill of Rights is the commonly-used term for the first ten amendments to the United States Constitution, which took effect on December 15, 1791. (Generically, the term "bill of rights" can also refer to any list of rights enjoyed by the citizens of a nation.) It restricts the ability of the government (though not private entities) to impose and enforce laws on the general populace and was originally intended to protect individuals from a strong central government. Among its protections are freedom of speech, freedom of religion, and freedom of the press. It includes many of the basic due process rights afforded defendants in criminal trials, including the right to a trial by a jury of peers, protection against unreasonable search and seizure, and protection against self-incrimination.

Application to Criminal Justice at the State Level

The Bill of Rights was intended by the Founding Fathers to apply only to the federal government and not to the individual state governments. After the Civil War, however, attempts were made to restrict the power of the states, and with the ratification of the Fourteenth Amendment to the US Constitution in 1868 the due process rights that applied to the federal government were extended to state governments as well. (There is some question as to whether this amendment was intended to extend other provisions of the Bill of Rights to the states in addition to due process rights.) It took a century for the Supreme Court to fully define exactly how these rights were to be applied on a state level.

Fourth Amendment to the US Constitution

The Fourth Amendment protects against unreasonable search and seizure. The text of the amendment states that private property may not be searched without a warrant issued for "probable cause" and that the warrant must specify the location, property or person to be searched. In addition, it guarantees that no one may be arrested without a justifiable reason. The meaning of the Fourth Amendment has been refined by the Supreme Court when it ruled in 1914 that any evidence acquired by authorities in violation of the amendment must be excluded during a trial. This is known as the exclusionary rule. Subsequent Courts have both broadened and narrowed Fourth amendment protections. In 1984, under Chief Justice Warren Burger, the Court ruled that evidence need not be excluded if police obtained it in "good faith" as a result of misinformation. The exclusionary rule also does not apply to evidence presented before a grand jury.

FIFTH AMENDMENT TO THE US CONSTITUTION

The Fifth Amendment protects against self-incrimination and double jeopardy. It also guarantees that certain "infamous" crimes, including murder, can come to trial only after indictment has been returned by a grand jury. The right against self-incrimination means that defendants in criminal cases cannot be compelled to testify against themselves. Protection against double jeopardy means that no one can be forced to stand trial twice for the same crime (though this has been interpreted in such a way as to allow someone to be tried for the same crime in both state and federal courts). In the cases Escobedo vs. Illinois (1964) and Miranda vs. Arizona (1966), the Supreme Court ruled that under the Fifth Amendment, the police must tell a suspect that they have "the right to remain silent" to protect them against self-incrimination. This is part of what has come to be known as a "Miranda warning."

SIXTH AMENDMENT TO THE US CONSTITUTION

The Sixth Amendment guarantees:

- The right to counsel -- All defendants in a criminal trial are guaranteed a lawyer and must be provided one by the government if unable to provide one for themselves.
- The right to a speedy and public trial -- The government may not force the accused to remain in jail before trial for an unreasonably long time, although the requirements of due process and the need of the state to prepare a case must be taken into account. The trial must be made available for public scrutiny, unless making the trial public leads to prejudicial publicity and undue embarrassment to those involved.
- The right to an impartial jury -- A jury of citizens must be available in all criminal trials and ideally this jury should be composed of a cross-section of the community in which the crime occurred. In practice, the jury is usually chosen randomly from the community, and jurors can be excluded after being questioned by lawyers for the prosecution and the defense.

EIGHTH AMENDMENT TO THE US CONSTITUTION

The Eighth Amendment guarantees against:

- Excessive bail -- This is not a guarantee that all accused criminals be allowed to go free on bail while their cases are awaiting trial, but a guarantee that the bail not be excessive. In certain jurisdictions, bail is not allowed for certain crimes, and judges can refuse to set bail for suspects who may be dangerous if released.
- Excessive fines -- The prohibition against excessive fines includes, according to a 1998 Supreme Court decision, a guarantee against excessive forfeiture of property.
- Cruel and unusual punishment -- This was a reaction against punishments used in Europe at the time the Constitution was written and has been variously interpreted over the years. Attempts have been made to have the death penalty ruled unconstitutional under this amendment, but these have met with limited success.

FOURTEENTH AMENDMENT TO THE US CONSTITUTION

Section 1 of the Fourteenth Amendment applies the guarantees of procedural due process provided by the Constitution to the states. Previously due process had applied only in federal trials, but beginning with this amendment began to apply on the state and local levels. The way in which this due process clause has been interpreted in the courts has changed considerably since the ratification of this amendment in 1868. It was not until the 1932, for instance, that the Supreme Court ruled in Powell vs. Alabama that courts needed to supply lawyers for indigent defendants, and it wasn't until the late 1960s that the Court under Chief Justice Warren Burger ruled that all constitutional guarantees of due process applied to the states.

SUBSTANTIVE DUE PROCESS

Substantive due process is the idea that the due process rights conferred by the Fifth and Fourteenth Amendments to the US Constitution include not just procedural rights of due process, but the entire philosophy of individual liberty that underlies due process. Specifically, it deals not with the procedures used to determine whether an individual has broken the law, but the substance of the laws themselves. Under substantive due process, courts have ruled that laws binding on US Citizens may not be vague or capricious, that they must spell out precisely the acts that they prohibit and the persons to which they apply, and that individuals accused of breaking the law must be made aware of what law they have broken and be given a chance to publicly defend themselves.

PROCEDURAL DUE PROCESS

Procedural due process concerns itself with the specific procedures under which individuals may be accused of breaking the law and the procedures that are used to establish their guilt and to set punishment. They include the right to be given notice of the proceedings that will determine guilt and the right to defend against the accusations in an impartial hearing. Specifically, the courts have ruled that these procedures must be applied before the government can take the life, liberty, or property of an accused person. The more severe the potential penalty, the more rigorously fair the process of deciding guilt must be.

SEARCH AND SEIZURE

Evidence gathering is an essential law enforcement tool. Evidence is necessary to prove that a crime has taken place and to identify the perpetrator. Evidence is generally presented in court to prove that the accused is guilty of the crime of which he or she has been accused. Evidence is obtained through search, generally of a suspect's property, and through seizing property believed to be relevant to the case. However, the Fourth Amendment to the United States Constitution specifically protects against unreasonable search and seizure. Thus, certain rules of due process must be followed by law enforcement officers in obtaining evidence. For instance, a search warrant should be obtained from a judge before private property is searched, and there must be probable cause that the search will lead to obtaining relevant evidence. However, under certain conditions a warrantless search may be performed.

SEARCH WARRANT

A search warrant is a court order from a judge, obtained by a law enforcement officer, allowing the officer to search an individual's person or property for the purpose of seizing evidence showing that a crime has been committed. To obtain a search warrant, it is necessary to show probable cause for its use. A search may be performed without a warrant if the individual consents or if certain circumstances exist, such as fear that the evidence may be destroyed before a warrant can be obtained or if the search is performed in the course of hot pursuit.

PROBABLE CAUSE

Probable cause is fact-based evidence that provides reasonable belief that a crime has been committed and that a search is justified to find further evidence. Probable cause does not provide certainty that the crime has been committed nor does it necessarily represent sufficient evidence to obtain a conviction, but it must suggest a reasonable belief that a crime may have been committed. Probable cause is necessary to obtain a search warrant. The United States Supreme Court has ruled on multiple occasions as to what constitutes probable cause. Currently, it is based on the "totality of circumstances" surrounding the crime.

Indianapolis v. Edmond

In the 2000 Supreme Court case Indianapolis v. Edmond, the court considered the circumstances under which law enforcement officers can perform searches without a reasonable suspicion of wrongdoing. At issue were police roadblocks and the use of trained dogs to detect illegal drugs. The right of the police to conduct roadblocks had already been established, but the court had specified that searches performed as a result of these roadblocks must "serve special needs, beyond the normal need for law enforcement." In this case, the court found that a "general interest in crime control" without a specific target or rationale was not sufficient to justify such roadblocks.

Stop-and-Frisk Search

A stop-and-frisk search can occur during a field interrogation, when law enforcement officers have stopped someone on suspicion of committing a crime. The Supreme Court has ruled that five conditions must be met before a stop-and-frisk search may be performed on a suspect in order for the search to be constitutionally valid in the absence of a warrant:

1. The officer must have reasonable grounds for suspecting that a crime has occurred or is in the process of occurring.
2. The person being searched must be armed and dangerous.
3. The investigating officer must identify him- or herself as such.
4. Reasonable inquiry must be made in advance of the search.
5. There must be reasonable evidence (and no evidence to the contrary) that the officer's safety is endangered.

These rules were established by the Supreme Court decision in the case Terry v. Ohio (1968).

Fruit of the Poisonous Tree Doctrine

The fruit of the poisonous tree (a term from the Gospel of Matthew) doctrine holds that evidence obtained via illegal search and seizure -- that is, search and seizure that does not meet the rules of due process as established by the US Constitution and the rulings of the US Supreme Court -- cannot be used against a subject in court. It is a form of the exclusionary rule, which is based on Fourth Amendment prohibitions against unreasonable search and seizure. The rule does not necessarily apply if it can be shown that the evidence would have been obtained eventually even if the illegal search and seizure had not taken place. (This is known as the "inevitable discovery" exception.)

J.E.B. v. Alabama

In the 1994 Supreme Court case J.E.B. v. Alabama, the high court considered the issue of whether lawyers can make a peremptory challenge purely on the basis of the sex of a prospective juror. A peremptory challenge is made during the voir dire, when jurors are being selected for a case. Generally, either the defense or prosecution can reject a certain number of potential jurors without giving a reason. In this case, however, the court ruled that gender-based peremptory challenges violate Fourteenth Amendment guarantees of equal protection under the law. Earlier, in Batson v. Kentucky, the court had ruled that race alone could not be used in a peremptory challenge. This ruling extended that earlier ruling to the sex of the juror as well.

Batson v. Kentucky

In the 1986 Supreme Court case Batson v. Kentucky, the high court considered the issue of whether lawyers can make a peremptory challenge, which rejects a potential juror from being empanelled, on the basis of race. In this case, an African-American man had been convicted of burglary by an all-white jury after all potential black jury members had been removed by peremptory challenges. The case was appealed on the belief that it violated Sixth Amendment guarantees that a jury will represent a cross-section of the community, as well as Fourteenth Amendment guarantees of equal protection under the law. The court agreed. This protection was extended to peremptory challenges on the basis of sex by the later J.E.B. v Alabama ruling.

Hurtado v. California

In the 1884 Supreme Court Hurtado v. California, a convicted murderer appealed his case on the grounds that his rights to due process had been violated because an indictment had not been handed down by a grand jury. The high court ruled that, although the Fourteenth Amendment extended due process rights to state trials, this did not include the right to a grand jury. Although state constitutions can guarantee the right to a grand jury for certain crimes, this is considered optional, despite constitutional requirements for grand jury indictments in federally-prosecuted capital trials.

Writ of Mandamus

A writ of mandamus is a legal document by which a higher court orders a lower court or a government to correct flawed actions or to perform a duty. (The term "mandamus" is from a Latin expression meaning "we demand [or command]".) The writ of mandamus is authorized by the Judiciary Act of 1789. It is used by the higher court when the lower court has acted outside its jurisdiction or been influenced by considerations that are not part of the case. It is used to redress injuries caused by the courts themselves.

Monroe v. Pape

In the 1961 Supreme Court case Monroe v. Pape, an African-American family had sued the City of Chicago for alleged civil rights violations under Section 1983 of the Civil Rights Act of 1871 (the so-called Ku Klux Klan Act), which allowed civil proceedings against state officials in civil rights cases. The court upheld the right of private citizens to bring suit against government officials, though it dismissed the idea that cities themselves could not be sued, a ruling that was overturned by the later Monell v. Department of Social Services of the City of New York.

Lambert v. California

In the 1957 Supreme Court case Lambert v. California, the court addressed the issue of whether there are circumstances in which the rule of thumb "ignorance of the law is no excuse" does not apply. In this particular case a felon, Lambert, was convicted of failing to register with the state of California, an action she was legally required to perform within five days. She appealed the case on the grounds that she was not aware of the law. Although this is not generally regarded as justification for not obeying local statutes, the high court ruled that in such "notice offenses," where inaction rather than action is involved, a standard of "probability of awareness" must be applied -- that is, the probability that the offender would actually be aware of the statute needs to be taken into account. In Lambert's case, there was no likelihood that she would have been aware that such a law existed.

Prompt Arraignment

The Supreme Court has long insisted that persons suspected of committing a crime must be charged promptly after being detained. The intent is to prevent the government from using detention itself along with extended interrogation lasting for several days as a means of extracting a confession (an interrogation method sometimes referred to as "the third degree"), since such a confession would violate due process. A 6-hour limit on pre-arraignment interrogations has been imposed by the courts; however, confessions obtained after this period of time are still admissible in court if a judge rules that the delay was reasonable.

Carroll Doctrine

The Carroll Doctrine comes from the Supreme Court decision in the 1925 case Carroll v. United States, in which the appellant claimed that his conviction for illegal transportation of alcoholic beverages was based on an illegal search of his automobile. The Court ruled that it is not necessary to obtain a search warrant in order to seize evidence from an automobile because the mobility of automobiles makes it too easy for illegal goods and other evidence of a crime to be moved out of the jurisdiction in which the warrant would be valid. Further rulings extended this principle to parked cars and to cars that have been seized and impounded by the police prior to the search, even though the latter vehicles were not likely to be moved out of the jurisdiction.

United States v. Calandra

In the 1974 Supreme Court case United States v. Calandra, the high court ruled that the exclusionary principle, under which evidence obtained illegally is not admissible in criminal trials, does not apply to grand jury proceedings. In this case, the FBI had used a search warrant later determined to have been issued without probable cause to seize evidence against John Calandra. The evidence was used by a grand jury to subpoena Calandra, who then asked that the illegal evidence be suppressed. The case was eventually appealed to the Supreme Court, which ruled that the evidence could be presented to the grand jury despite having been seized in violation of Fourth Amendment protection against illegal search and seizure. The court held that "[t]he exclusionary rule...is a judicially created remedy designed to safeguard Fourth Amendment rights generally through its deterrent effect on future unlawful police conduct, rather than a personal constitutional right of the party aggrieved."

Random spot checks of automobiles

Random spot checks occur when police officers stop cars and check registrations for no probable cause other than the offhand possibility that the drivers might be guilty of something. Sometimes these checks, especially when held at certain hours of the night and on certain days of the week, will result in the apprehension of a criminal. Such spot checks have been discouraged by the Supreme Court, on the grounds that searches at police discretion can be discriminatory and violate the Fourth Amendment. However, the Supreme Court has allowed spot checks that are not made at officer discretion -- for instance, certain checks where all cars are stopped and searched at a roadblock in order to reduce immediate road hazards such as drunken drivers or to protect the US borders from illegal immigration.

Fresh pursuit

Fresh pursuit, also known as hot pursuit, occurs when police are following a suspect believed to be escaping the scene of a crime. Fresh pursuit must occur without reasonable delay after a crime is believed to have been committed. Warrantless search and seizure is permitted during fresh pursuit, as is warrantless arrest. Police departments have, however, made attempts to regulate fresh pursuit by vehicle, which can endanger the public safety, though generally the wisdom of vehicular pursuit is left to police discretion. Some police forces have officer training programs that attempt to establish safe methods of pursuit.

Plain view doctrine

The "plain view" doctrine derives from the 1968 Supreme Court case Harris v. United States, in which it was ruled that a police officer may seize any evidence that is in his or her "plain view" without a warrant, as long as the officer has not entered the area illegally and is not already performing an illegal search. Evidence acquired in this fashion may be used in court. This doctrine has been extended under the protective sweep doctrine, which holds that law enforcement officers are justified, during the course of an arrest on private premises, in searching those premises for individuals who may threaten the safety of the officers or of any evidence that may exist on those premises. Any evidence in "plain view" during such a sweep may be seized without a warrant.

SPEEDY TRIAL

The right to a speedy trial is guaranteed by the Sixth Amendment to the US Constitution. It was intended to protect the accused against indefinite incarceration by the government. The concept of speedy trial has never been precisely defined and has become problematic over the years, because high court interpretations of constitutional due process have added an increasing number of procedures that must be followed in a criminal prosecution and because of the increasingly crowded court dockets in some jurisdictions. Evidence-gathering periods and the amount of time necessary for attorneys on both sides to prepare their cases have grown over the years, making speediness a relative concept. The Supreme Court has generally defined a speedy trial as a trial that takes place in a "reasonable" amount of time without unreasonable delays. In some cases, local statutes place a specific limit on the duration of a case.

RIGHT TO TRIAL BY JURY

The right to trial by jury is a provision of Article III of the United States Constitution, which reads, "The trial of all crimes, except in cases of impeachment, shall be by jury." This concept, that an accused person must be judged by their "peers," derives from English common law and dates back to the Magna Carta in 1215. The Supreme Court has imposed two important requirements on trial by jury: The jury must consist of 12 people and the verdict must be unanimous. (If the jury proves unable to reach a unanimous verdict, a mistrial is declared.) These rights originally applied only to federal trials, but were extended to state and local trials by the Supreme Court in the 1968 case Duncan v. Louisiana. In state trials, however, the jury may consist of fewer than 12 people.

DOUBLE JEOPARDY

Double jeopardy is placing the same person on trial more than once for the same crime and is prohibited by the Fifth Amendment to the United States Constitution, which reads, "Nor shall any person be subject for the same offense to be twice put in jeopardy of life or limb." The Supreme Court has provided a number of interpretations and qualifications of this right. For instance, a person may be tried twice for the same crime if one time is in federal court and the second is in a state court (though not in both a city court and state court). This is called dual sovereignty. A person may also be tried twice for the same crime if the first trial is declared a mistrial.

COMPULSORY PROCESS CLAUSE

The compulsory process clause of the Sixth Amendment to the United States Constitution provides the right to defendants to compel witnesses to testify at a trial via subpoena. Specifically, the amendment states that "the accused shall enjoy the right to have compulsory process for obtaining witnesses in his favor." Thus, these are generally witnesses expected to bolster the case presented by the defense, who are called to the stand as the defense presents its case. This right is in contradiction to English common law principles, but is considered essential to a proper defense under the US criminal justice system.

HABEAS CORPUS

Habeas corpus is a Latin phrase meaning "you have the body." A defendant jailed in a criminal case may file a writ of habeas corpus demanding that a judge institute a civil procedure to determine whether they are being detained under proper due process. Habeas corpus is recognized as a fundamental right in protecting individual citizens against arbitrary actions on the part of the government. Nonetheless, the right to file a writ of habeas corpus can and has been suspended at various times in US history -- during the Civil War, for instance, and as part of the war on terror -- allowing the government to imprison individuals indefinitely without due process.

Weems v. United States

In the 1910 Supreme Court case Weems v. United States, the court considered the issue of whether an unreasonably long prison sentence can be considered cruel and unusual punishment. The petitioner had been sentenced to 15 years for the crime of falsifying a government document. The high court concluded that the sentence, which included "hard and painful labor" and the frequent chaining of the defendant, violated Eighth Amendment guarantees and was therefore unconstitutional. The decision was made despite the fact that it involved punishments not known when the Constitution was written, thereby confirming the flexibility of the Constitution and its ability to accommodate circumstances not foreseen by the founding fathers.

Warren Court

The term Warren Court refers to the Supreme Court in the period 1953 to 1969 during the tenure of Chief Justice Earl Warren. This period in Supreme Court history was notable for a number of significant changes in the way constitutional rights were interpreted and significantly extended the due process rights of criminal suspects and defendants. Such landmark Supreme Court cases as Brown v. Board of Education, Mapp v. Ohio, and Miranda v. Arizona occurred during this period. Significant rulings by the Warren Court were made not only in the area of criminal justice, but also in the area of civil rights. Warren Court rulings were mostly in accord with the Due Process Model of criminal justice.

Burger Court

The term Burger Court is used to describe the Supreme Court under Warren Burger, who was Chief Justice from 1969 to 1986. The Burger Court succeeded the Warren Court and is sometimes seen as a conservative reaction to it. Burger Court decisions on due process were in accord with the Crime Control Model of criminal justice, which views the punishment of criminals to be more important than the rights of the accused. The Burger Court placed a de facto moratorium on the death penalty in 1972 with its ruling that capital punishment was imposed arbitrarily and inconsistently, but this ended with the decision in the 1976 case Gregg v. Georgia.

Fare v. Michael C

In the 1979 Supreme Court case Fare v. Michael C., the high court dealt with the issue of whether the Sixth Amendment right to counsel applied to juvenile offenders. The court determined that juvenile offenders had such rights even in juvenile court, but that it was necessary for the court itself to safeguard this right against the possibility that an underage offender may have been coerced into waiving the right to counsel by interrogators. In this case, it was determined that the young offender, accused of murder, had in fact waived his rights.

North Carolina v. Alford

In the 1970 Supreme Court case North Carolina v. Alford, the high court dealt with the issue of whether a defendant can make a guilty plea while still maintaining innocence -- for instance, when the plea is being made in return for some form of leniency. The court agreed that, yes, a judge may accept a plea of guilty while the defendant does not admit guilt. This has become known as an Alford plea and is similar to a plea of nolo contendere or "no contest." The defendant admits in effect that, in spite of his or her claim of innocence, there is enough evidence for the jury to reach a verdict of guilty.

Wyoming v. Houghton

In the 1925 case Carroll v. United States, the Supreme Court ruled that automobiles represented an exception to Fourth Amendment protections against unreasonable search and seizure in that automobiles could be moved quickly from the jurisdiction of a police officer and there was no time for a warrant to be obtained against that eventuality. Thus, if probable cause for a search existed, it could be performed without a warrant. In the 1999 case Wyoming v. Houghton, the court considered whether this exception extended to a purse or other container being held by a passenger of the vehicle. In this case, the defendant (Houghton) was arrested after a police search that found illegal drugs in her purse. The high court ruled that probable cause had been present (drug paraphernalia had been visible) and the warrantless search of the purse had been reasonable.

Brown v. Mississippi

In the Supreme Court case Brown v. Mississippi (1936), the Court established that confessions obtained through coercion are not admissible in state courts, extending Fifth Amendment protections against self-incriminations to state trials. In this case, three black men suspected of murder were repeatedly tortured until they confessed. A conviction obtained on the basis of this confession and upheld by the Mississippi Supreme Court was finally overturned by the United States Supreme Court. This led to a number of instances in which cases involving coerced confessions were reversed in the high court.

Weeks v. United States

Weeks v. United States was one of several Supreme Court cases that served to establish the use of the exclusionary rule, which holds that evidence acquired in violation of Fourth Amendment protections against unreasonable search and seizure is not admissible in court. The case, from 1914, concerned a United States marshal who had searched the home of a suspect without a warrant. The Federal government refused to return property seized during this search to its owner and used them to obtain a conviction during the trial. The Supreme Court overturned the conviction despite the strong probability that the defendant was guilty because of the Fourth Amendment violations. The case established the applicability of the exclusionary rule in Federal trials where evidence has been seized by Federal agents.

United States v. Leon

In the 1984 Supreme Court case United States v. Leon, the high court considered that there could be possible exceptions to the Exclusionary Rule, which holds that evidence obtained through illegal search and seizure cannot be used in court. In this case, a search warrant had been obtained based on a police informant's tip concerning a pair of suspected drug dealers. The warrant was later found to be invalid, but the lower court ruled that the evidence could be used anyway because the warrant had been obtained in "good faith," with no intent to violate the Fourth Amendment. The Supreme Court upheld this ruling, stating that the good faith exception was valid because the warrant had been issued through a mistake of the judge issuing it, rather than flawed police work.

Inevitable Discovery Exception

The "inevitable discovery" exception is an exception to the exclusionary rule (which states that evidence obtained through illegal search and seizure is inadmissible in court) articulated by the Supreme Court in the cases Brewer v. Williams (1977) and Nix v. Williams (1984). In the earlier case, a man had abducted and murdered a young girl. The police found her body on the basis of questioning that was performed without an attorney present. Initially, the Supreme Court ruled that the evidence was inadmissible, but in the later case agreed with an attorney who argued that the discovery of the girl's body had been "inevitable" because search teams were nearby and would have reached the site had police not reached it first. Thus the evidence was deemed admissible, on the grounds that it would have been discovered even without the confession.

Wolf v. Colorado

Wolf v. Colorado (1949) was one of several Supreme Court cases that served to establish the use of the exclusionary rule in criminal trials. In this case, evidence had been obtained against a defendant accused of performing illegal abortions through police questioning of the patients whose names appeared in the defendant's appointment book. However, the appointment book had been acquired through a warrantless search that was declared unconstitutional. The Supreme Court refused to declare this evidence inadmissible, despite the earlier decision in Weeks v. United States where a conviction was overturned because it was based on illegally seized evidence, because in Wolf the conviction had taken place in a state rather than federal court. At this time the high court had not yet extended the exclusionary rule to state trials, though they would do so in the 1961 case Mapp v. Ohio.

Mapp v. Ohio

In the 1961 Supreme Court case Mapp v. Ohio, the high court finally extended the exclusionary rule, which states that illegally-seized evidence is inadmissible in a criminal trial, to the state level. Previously this principle had been held, in Weeks vs. United States, to apply in federal trials. In Mapp, Cleveland police had arrested Dollree Mapp for possessing allegedly pornographic materials. These materials had been obtained by the police during a warrantless search of her house. (Mapp was suspected of harboring a fugitive.) The Ohio Supreme Court upheld the decision, allowing the use of the evidence seized during the search at the trial, but the Supreme Court overturned the decision, declaring that illegally-seized evidence was just as inadmissible at the state level as at the federal.

Exceptions to the Exclusionary Rule

The exclusionary rule, which holds that illegally seized evidence is not inadmissible in court, was fully established by the 1961 Supreme Court case Mapp v. Ohio, but in subsequent years the high court has found several exceptions to the rule. For instance, according to the Court the exclusionary rule does not apply during grand jury proceedings. Federal courts are not required to use a writ of habeas corpus to enforce the exclusionary rule at the state level. And the Court has established good faith exceptions to the rule such that evidence remains admissible if police genuinely believe that they have obtained a valid warrant that later turns out to be invalid because of certain technical errors.

Mempa v. Ray

In the 1967 Supreme Court case Mempa v. Ray, the court dealt with the issue of whether delayed sentencing can be imposed without counsel present. The petitioner had been put on probation for the offense of joyriding (stealing a car for temporary use) and had his probation revoked two years later when it was found that he had been involved in a burglary. He had no lawyer present nor was he asked if he wanted a lawyer. He later filed a writ of habeas corpus, alleging that he had been denied the right to counsel. The Supreme Court agreed in a ruling that established the right to have counsel present during probation revocation hearings where a delayed sentence is imposed.

Twining v. New Jersey

In the 1908 Supreme Court case Twining v. New Jersey, the defendant had been convicted in a trial where the judge had suggested that the jury could regard the fact that the defendant had refused to testify as a possible indicator of his guilt. The case was appealed to the high court on the premise that the defendant's Fifth Amendment protection against self-incrimination had been violated. The court, while not disagreeing that this represented forced self-incrimination, nonetheless held that protection against self-incrimination was "not fundamental in due process of law," effectively establishing that Fifth Amendment protections did not apply in state courts. This principle was reversed in 1936 in Brown v. Mississippi, though protection against self-incrimination was not fully extended to defendants in state trials until the 1964 case Malloy v. Hogan.

Gagnon v. Scarpelli

In the 1973 Supreme Court case Gagnon v. Scarpelli, the court dealt with issues surrounding the violation of terms of probation. The defendant, Gerald Scarpelli, had been sent to prison for associating with criminals who had committed a burglary with his assistance while he was on probation for a different crime. The determination to revoke his probation was based on his own confession. Three years later, Scarpelli appealed the case, alleging that the confession had been obtained under duress and thus violated his rights. The court ruled that Scarpelli should have been given a hearing when his probation was rescinded, thus extending rights that had been earlier given to parolees in Morrisey v. Brewer.

Lawrence v. Texas

In the 2003 Supreme Court case Lawrence v. Texas, the court dealt with the issue of laws that criminalize homosexual acts. The petitioners had been arrested for engaging in consensual same-sex anal intercourse, which under Texas law was a criminal offense. Arguments before the court alleged that this violated Fourteenth Amendment guarantees of equal protection in that the same activity was not prohibited for heterosexual couples as well as Fourteenth Amendment guarantees of due process. The court agreed, holding that the petitioners' due process rights had been violated. This decision had a wide-ranging effect on such sodomy laws across the United States, effectively declaring them unconstitutional.

Powell v. Alabama

In the 1932 Supreme Court case Powell v. Alabama, a group of eight black males (known popularly as The Scottsboro Boys) had been convicted of rape in a trial in Alabama and sentenced to death, despite medical evidence that no rape had in fact taken place. One of the convictions had been overturned by the Supreme Court of Alabama. The case was appealed to the Supreme Court on the grounds that the defendants had been denied Fourteenth Amendment rights to due process and had not been given a fair and impartial trial. The major finding in the Supreme Court's decision was that the defendants had been denied the right to counsel. It was the first major case establishing the right of poor defendants in state trials to be represented by counsel and to have that counsel provided for them by the state.

Injunctive relief

Injunctive relief is requested through an injunction, a form of court order demanding that someone stop doing something. In criminal law, injunctive relief is often the result of a writ of habeas corpus filed by a prisoner requesting the cessation of certain conditions accompanying imprisonment, such as unsanitary facilities, illegal actions by prison authorities, or even the length of the prison stay, or a refusal to grant parole. The injunctive relief frequently involves an alleged violation of due process, such as a violation of Eighth Amendment guarantees against cruel and unusual punishment.

Johnson v. Zerbst

In the 1938 Supreme Court case Johnson v. Zerbst, the defendant (Johnson) had been convicted in federal court of passing counterfeit money while serving as his own attorney. The Supreme Court reversed the lower court's decision, determining that the defendant had been deprived of his right to counsel and had "not competently and intelligently waived his constitutional right." The significance of Johnson v. Zerbst is that it was the first Supreme Court case to establish that all defendants in federal trials had a right to counsel (and not just those who could not afford that counsel). However, it did not extend this right to defendants in state trials, though the earlier Powell v. Alabama had established that poor defendants in a state trial have the right to have counsel supplied by the state.

Betts v. Brady

In the 1942 Supreme Court case Betts v. Brady, the defendant (Betts) had been denied counsel during his trial for robbery in Maryland. The Supreme Court refused to overturn the conviction, stating that in state court cases the right to counsel was only one element of a fair trial and was not necessarily fundamental to the defendant's Sixth Amendment rights. However, Justice Hugo Black wrote in his dissent that a "practice cannot be reconciled with 'common and fundamental ideas of fairness and right,' which subjects innocent men to increased dangers of conviction merely because of their poverty." This presaged future opinions by the high court, which essentially reversed itself on this issue in Gideon v. Wainwright.

Palko v. Connecticut

In the 1937 Supreme Court case Palko v. Connecticut, the court considered whether the Fourteenth Amendment's extension of due process rights to the states includes protections against double jeopardy. In this case, the defendant was found guilty of the murder of two police officers and sentenced to life in prison. The state appealed the case, retrying the defendant, after which he was sentenced to death. The case was then appealed by the defendant on the grounds that the two trials violated Fifth Amendment protections against double jeopardy. The court ruled that the Fourteenth Amendment did not protect against double jeopardy. Justice Benjamin Cardozo wrote in his decision that the Fourteenth Amendment only covered those rights that were "of the very essence of a scheme of ordered liberty." This ruling was reversed in the later Benton v. Maryland.

Klopfer v. North Carolina

In the 1967 Supreme Court Case Klopfer v. North Carolina, the defendant claimed that his Sixth Amendment right to a speedy trial had been violated by a prosecutor who had filed a "nolle prosequi with leave," which allowed the prosecutor to re-prosecute the case at any time. The Supreme Court held that this was indeed a violation of the petitioner's Sixth Amendment rights. The significance of the case is that it established that Sixth Amendment rights not only applied at the federal level, but also at the state level. This was one of a number of Supreme Court rulings that extended due process rights to state criminal trials.

Gideon v. Wainwright

In the 1963 Supreme Court case Gideon v. Wainwright, the defendant (Clarence Earl Gideon) had been convicted by the state of Florida of breaking and entering. The state court judge had refused to provide Gideon with counsel, though the indigent defendant was unable to afford one on his own. He defended himself, lost, and appealed his case to the Supreme Court from his prison cell. The high court overturned the lower court, declaring that the right to counsel was a fundamental right and that it could under no circumstances be denied. Furthermore, this right transcended income level and social class, and did not depend on the type of case. (The state of Florida had denied counsel to Gideon because it was not a capital case.) This case effectively overruled the earlier Betts v. Brady.

Argersinger v. Hamlin

In the 1972 Supreme Court case Argersinger v. Hamlin, the high court ruled that the right to counsel applied to all criminal defendants regardless of the type of crime of which they are accused, as long as the case is potentially punishable by a jail sentence. This ruling extended the right to counsel first put forth by the court in the earlier Gideon v. Wainwright to defendants who are not indigent. In its decision, the court found that "no accused may be deprived of his liberty as the result of any criminal prosecution, whether felony or misdemeanor, in which he was denied the assistance of counsel."

Barron v. Baltimore

In the 1833 Supreme Court case Barron v. Baltimore, the high court dealt with the issue of whether constitutional protections of due process apply at the state as well as the federal level. John Barron, a wharf owner in Baltimore, sued the city government for diverting a stream in such a way that it rendered his property unprofitable. He claimed that the city's actions violated his Fifth Amendment rights against having "private property...taken for public use, without just compensation." The court ruled that this provision of the Fifth Amendment was "intended solely as a limitation on the exercise of power by the government of the United States, and is not applicable to the legislation of the states," thereby denying defendants in state trials the same due process rights required in federal trials. This decision was essentially overturned by later high court decisions upholding Fourteenth Amendment rights guaranteeing due process on the state level.

Kyllo v. United States

In the 2001 Supreme Court case Kyllo v. United States, the high court dealt with the unusual problem of evidence gathering with the use of thermal-imaging devices and whether using such devices without a search warrant constitutes illegal search and seizure under the Fourth Amendment. In this case, thermal imaging was used to determine that marijuana was being grown in a suspect's house under heat-generating lights. The court ruled that the police had erred in not obtaining a warrant and declared the thermal-imaging evidence inadmissible.

Buck v. Bell

In the 1927 Supreme Court case Buck v. Bell, the high court ruled on the issue of eugenics, in this case the forced sterilization of individuals deemed to be unfit. A woman had been sterilized by order of a court because she was found to be mentally incompetent. The sterilization was performed under a Virginia statute that made such sterilization compulsory. The court upheld the lower court decision, ruling that it was in the interests of the state that such individuals not have children. In the later Skinner v. Oklahoma, the court ruled that sterilization could not be used as punishment for a crime, though they did not specifically overturn Buck v. Bell. Nonetheless, such sterilization laws have largely vanished.

Open fields doctrine

The "open fields" doctrine is an exception to protections against unreasonable search and seizure, similar to the plain view doctrine. It holds that there is no reasonable expectation of privacy in open fields surrounding a property, even if a No Trespassing sign has been posted. Evidence visible in such an area can be seized without a warrant. However, the Supreme Court makes an exception for the yard immediately around the house, an area called the curtilage. Nonetheless, the plain view doctrine holds for the curtilage inasmuch as evidence in plain sight within it can be reasonably seized, even if it is only visible from an airplane.

M'Naghten Rule

The M'Naghten Rule derives from an 1843 case before the British House of Lords in which the accused was acquitted of murder because he suffered from mental illness and was judged to be delusional at the time of the killing. The rule states that the accused must be "possessed of sufficient understanding when he committed the criminal act to know that it was wrong" in order to be held criminally responsible. A person who does "not know the nature or quality of the act, or did know what he was doing but did not know that it was wrong...is not responsible." The M'Naghten Rule was the beginning of the modern insanity defense, but came under criticism in the 20th century for not taking into account the modern understanding of mental illness.

DURHAM RULE

The Durham Rule derives from a 1954 case before the US Court of Appeals in the District of Columbia. It extended the M'Naghten rule, such that a defendant may be found not guilty if their actions were "the product of mental disease or defect." According to the judge, the M'Naghten rule depended on "an entirely obsolete and misleading conception of the nature of insanity." However, this ruling was overturned in 1972, and the Durham Rule has been used little since that time because it was judged to be overly broad, vague in its definition of mental illness, and because it puts too much emphasis on the testimony of expert witnesses.

BRAWNER RULE

The Brawner Rule derives from the 1972 case United States v. Brawner, in which it was argued that the earlier Durham Rule denied the jury an opportunity to determine the guilt of the defendant in cases involving an insanity plea. This violated the defendant's Sixth Amendment rights to trial by a jury of peers. Instead of leaving the question of the accused's mens rea to expert witnesses, the Brawner Rule allows the jury to decide whether or not a mental incapacity has affected the accused's ability to distinguish right from wrong.

FEDERAL BUREAU OF INVESTIGATION

The Federal Bureau of Investigation, more commonly known as the FBI and founded in 1887 as the Bureau of Investigation (BOI), is the major investigative arm of the federal government and is part of the United States Department of Justice. By statute, it combats "crimes against the United States." More specifically, it investigates federal crimes. The FBI's own description of its mission, posted on its web site, is to "protect and defend the United States against terrorist and foreign intelligence threats, to uphold and enforce the criminal laws of the United States, and to provide leadership and criminal justice services to federal, state, municipal, and international agencies and partners." This includes a number of more specific missions, such as:

- "Protect the United States against cyber-based attacks and high-technology crimes."
- "Combat public corruption at all levels."
- "Protect civil rights."
- "Combat major white-collar crime."
- "Combat significant violent crime."

BUREAU OF ALCOHOL, TOBACCO, FIREARMS AND EXPLOSIVES

The Bureau of Alcohol, Tobacco, Firearms and Explosives (ATF) is a government agency charged with investigating crimes involving illegally-produced, distributed and sold alcohol and tobacco; the illegal use, possession, manufacture and trafficking of firearms and explosives; and criminal acts of arson. It was founded in 1886, and though it has been under the direction of several government agencies over the years, it is currently part of the Department of Justice. On its web site, the ATF describes itself as "a unique law enforcement agency in the United States Department of Justice that protects our communities from violent criminals, criminal organizations, the illegal use and trafficking of firearms, the illegal use and storage of explosives, acts of arson and bombings, acts of terrorism, and the illegal diversion of alcohol and tobacco products."

Department of Homeland Security

The Department of Homeland Security is a department of the Federal government formed in the aftermath of the September 11, 2001, attacks on the World Trade Center and Pentagon. Its function is to protect the United States against domestic emergencies. These include emergencies caused by both terrorist acts and natural disasters. It incorporates a number of agencies that previously operated under other departments, including the Immigration and Naturalization Service, the US Coast Guard, the Federal Emergency Management Agency, the US Customs Service, and the Animal and Plant Health Inspection Service, the last two under the collective heading of US Customs and Border Protection.

Interpol

Interpol is an international police organization (the name is a contraction of International Criminal Police Organization) founded in 1923 that provides support for police organizations in most countries around the world and promotes cooperation among those organizations. Interpol can become directly involved in criminal cases that cross national borders, such as drug trafficking cases, but its major role is in record keeping. Interpol keeps a large database of crimes and of the names and records of international criminals that may be consulted by the police of member nations. Most countries, including the United States, are members of Interpol. The US National Central Bureau of Interpol is based in Washington, DC, and includes members of several American law enforcement organizations.

DEA

The Drug Enforcement Administration (DEA) is a largely independent branch of the Federal Bureau of Investigation (FBI) that enforces laws against drug trafficking and smuggling. On their web site, the DEA states that its mission is to " to enforce the controlled substances laws and regulations of the United States and bring to the criminal and civil justice system of the United States, or any other competent jurisdiction, those organizations and principal members of organizations, involved in the growing, manufacture, or distribution of controlled substances appearing in or destined for illicit traffic in the United States; and to recommend and support non-enforcement programs aimed at reducing the availability of illicit controlled substances on the domestic and international markets."

Federal Protective Service

The Federal Protective Service is in charge of enforcing the law in federally-owned and -leased buildings. It is a division of the United States Department of Homeland Security. The work of the FPS includes installing monitoring equipment in federal buildings and providing a visible security presence in those buildings to deter lawbreaking or terrorist acts. They also help devise emergency plans for those buildings. Before becoming part of Homeland Security, the FPS was part of Immigration and Customs Enforcement. For its work, the FPS often contracts out specific duties to private security firms.

Federal Air Marshal Service

The Federal Air Marshal Service, founded in 1963, provides security for civil aviation, both on flights and at the airport. It is part of the Transportation Security Administration. Federal Air Marshals do not wear distinctive uniforms but are essentially plain clothes officers, blending in with the other passengers on airplanes. They do carry guns, but are required to be unusually-proficient in the use of weapons to reduce the risk of injuring other passengers or the airplanes themselves. They are an important force against terrorists, particularly as terrorism involves the hijacking of airplanes.

US Coast Guard

The United States Coast Guard is a military organization that is also a law enforcement agency. It operates under both the Department of Homeland Security and the Department of the Navy. In peacetime, its search and rescue helps people in danger at sea or threatened by maritime weather and its National Response Center deals with oil spills and similar ecological emergencies at sea. But its major role in law enforcement is in enforcing drug laws, combating smuggling, and providing security for American shipping. It also enforces US maritime treaties. Coast Guard officers are uniformed and can carry firearms.

BIA

The Bureau of Indian Affairs (BIA) works with tribal police agencies on American Indian tribal lands within the United States. It is a division of the United States Department of the Interior. The BIA's law enforcement wing is the Office of Justice Services. According to the Bureau's Web site, it "[o]perates the Indian Police Academy," " [p]rovides emergency tactical response teams to reservations requiring assistance, or threatened with disruptions or civil disorder," "[c]onducts criminal investigations into criminal violations committed on reservations involving Federal, State, County, Local and Tribal codes" and "[d]irectly operates law enforcement programs for tribes who do not run their own programs."

IRS

The Internal Revenue Service (IRS) is responsible for collecting US income taxes, but it is also a law enforcement agency, responsible for enforcing laws related to the Internal Revenue Code. Law enforcement functions of the IRS are the responsibility of the IRS Criminal Investigation Division. The IRS can investigate cases of money laundering and cases involving the financial aspects of trafficking in illicit narcotics. Perhaps the most famous law enforcement case in IRS history involved the arrest of mobster Al Capone on charges of income tax evasion. According to its Web site, "Criminal Investigation must investigate and assist in the prosecution of those significant financial investigations that will generate the maximum deterrent effect, enhance voluntary compliance, and promote public confidence in the tax system."

Postal Inspection Service

The United States Postal Inspection Service (USPIS) is a division of the United States Postal Service (USPS). Its law enforcement mission includes the investigation of mail fraud and other forms of "criminal misuse of the mails." The USPIS was called on to investigate cases of anthrax being sent through the mail in the period immediately after the September 11, 2001, attacks. The USPIS works to protect mail carriers from attack and to investigate cases of mail theft. It also investigates cases of illicit drugs and child pornography being sent through US mail.

Secret Service

The Secret Service is a division of the United States Treasury Department. Its best-known law enforcement function is the protection of presidents of the United States and other dignitaries as necessary, but as part of the Treasury Department it also enforces laws against counterfeiting and fraud. In addition, according to the Secret Service web site, it "implements and evaluates prevention and response measures to guard against electronic crimes as well as other computer related fraud." It also investigates "access device fraud, identity theft, false identification fraud, bank fraud and check fraud; telemarketing fraud; telecommunications fraud (cellular and hard wire); computer fraud; fraud targeting automated payment systems and teller machines; direct deposit fraud; investigations of forgery, uttering, alterations, false impersonations or false claims involving US

Treasury Checks, US Saving Bonds, US Treasury Notes, Bonds and Bills; electronic funds transfer (EFT)."

United States Park Police

The National Park Service, a division of the United States Department of the Interior, manages all national parks in the United States along with designated conservation areas and the grounds of some national monuments. It also operates the United States Park Police, which has full police jurisdiction over all the lands operated by the Park Service. According to its web site, the Park Police force "provides highly trained and professional police officers to prevent and detect criminal activity, conduct investigations, apprehend individuals suspected of committing offenses against Federal, State and local laws, provide protection to the President of the United States and visiting dignitaries, and provide protective services to some of the most recognizable monuments and memorials in the world."

US CBP

US Customs and Border Protection (CBP) is a division of the United States Department of Homeland Security. It was formed in March 2003 and takes over many of the law enforcement functions of the now-nonexistent US Immigration and Naturalization Service. Its mission includes preventing illegal immigration and combating the smuggling of illicit drugs. The CBP plays an important role in protecting the United States from terrorism. It also plays a role in the regulation of trade and the protection of intellectual property rights.

Police

Frankpledge System

The frankpledge, or frith-borh, system was an early form of policing established in Medieval England. Under this system, 10-man groups known as "tythings" or "tithings" were formed and pledged to report any crimes that they became aware of. Over time this developed into a kind of citizen police force, in which ordinary people were drafted into the crime-fighting profession. These groups of citizens were directed by a constable, who could order them to perform tasks that included firefighting and lamplighting (which served to deter crime by lighting dark areas).

Political Era of American Police

In the period from 1840 to 1920, the American police were closely connected to American politics, especially to the "machine" style of politics, where tightly knit political organizations ran cities through systems of favors and payoffs that reinforced the presence and power of the organization. This is the period when the first American professional police forces were founded, and in many cases, they were both the product of these political machines and an enforcement arm that helped encourage supporters of the machine to report to the polls on Election Day. These police forces were mostly organized as foot patrols and provided public services such as running homeless shelters. The maintenance of public order was important for the police during this era and was emphasized over fighting crime. In the American Southeast during this same period, police forces were developed in response to a fear of slave uprisings. In the West, police forces were modeled on the English sheriff system.

Professional Model Era of American Police

In the period from 1920 to 1970, American police evolved under the influence of the Progressive movement, which felt that law enforcement should exist for the good of all and not just politicians, as was the case during the earlier "political era" of American policing. In addition, the emphasis in law enforcement gradually moved away from maintaining order to fighting crime. This meant less emphasis on community service, but also less conflict of interest and potential for corruption. This period also introduced new technologies to crime-fighting. The greater emphasis that the police were placing on crime fighting during this era helped establish support for the police from ordinary citizens. However, political changes (such as the civil rights movement) often conflicted with the role of police in this period, and to some extent the effectiveness of the police at fighting crime turned out to be illusory.

Community-Policing Era of American Police

From the 1970s to the present day, the focus in police work began moving back to where it had been in the 19th century, toward community service and preservation of order. Studies in this period showed that the crime-fighting success of police in the mid-20th century had been overstated, and money being invested in additional neighborhood patrols and rapid response was not well spent. Instead, it was suggested that forming ties between the police and the residents of the neighborhoods that they protected would prevent situations that might evolve into crimes and prevent crime before it happened. Further, the "broken windows" theory of crime suggested that maintaining order in a neighborhood would prevent an atmosphere conducive to crime from developing, making order maintenance into a form of crime-fighting.

THE PINKERTON AGENCY

The Pinkerton National Detective Agency was a privately run security firm founded in 1850 and based in Chicago. It was run by Alan Pinkerton and took the motto "We Never Sleep." After uncovering a post-Civil War plot to assassinate Abraham Lincoln, the Pinkertons became the most famous police agency in the United States and for a time were larger than the US Army. They were hired to guard railroads in the American West of the 19th century, and their services were frequently engaged in violent management-labor disputes. They pursued such outlaws as Jesse James and Cole Younger, as well as Butch Cassidy & the Sundance Kid (Robert Leroy Parker and Harry Lombaugh) and the other members of their Hole in the Wall Gang. Perhaps their most enduring legacy is that they coined the term "private eye."

VIGILANTE JUSTICE

Vigilante justice was a well-established tradition on the American frontier of the 18th and 19th centuries and consisted not only of impromptu lynch mobs, but organized paramilitary groups such as the East Texas Regulators and the California Vigilante Committees. The better established vigilante groups had their own constitutions and organizational hierarchies. Some groups would even provide trials for captured outlaws, though these trials were not sanctioned by statute. By the 20th century, vigilantism had largely disappeared in the United States, but a few groups, such as the Guardian Angels, have persisted until the present day and maintain an uneasy coexistence with the police.

POSSE

A posse, from the Latin term posse comitatus ("power of the country"), is a group of citizens pressed into service by a sheriff for purposes of law enforcement. The concept of the posse arose in the ninth century Anglo-Saxon England of Alfred the Great. In the United States it was a common means of enforcing criminal law in frontier regions, which moved slowly westward during the 19th century. Members of a sheriff's posse served a purpose much like that of modern police forces and were expected to respond when summoned by the sheriff.

SHERIFF

A sheriff is the main agent of law enforcement in a county. The tradition of sheriffs (from the term "shire reeve") comes from medieval England and has been adopted in several other English-speaking countries, including the United States. During the 19th century, sheriffs were the main law enforcement officers west of the Mississippi River in the US and commonly held a number of official positions in addition to their law enforcement duties. These jobs could include tax collector, election official, and treasurer. In many areas the sheriff was an elected official. The sheriff could raise a posse of citizens to help in his duties if few or no deputies were available.

WOMEN ON THE US POLICE FORCE

HISTORIC ROLE

The first female police officer in the United States, hired in 1910, was Alice Stebbins Wells of Los Angeles, who worked as a plain clothes officer. Prior to that, women in the police force were restricted to clerical and social work positions. Female police officers remained relatively rare until the passage of the Civil Rights Act of 1964, which prohibited "discrimination on the basis of race, religion, creed, color, sex, or national origin with regard to hiring, compensation, terms, conditions and privileges of employment," and the Equal Opportunity Act of 1972. These acts still allowed employers to discriminate on the basis of an individual's qualifications for a job, but the employer is given the burden of proving that the discrimination is based on "bona-fide occupational qualifications." Even so, female police officers were often given different assignments than male officers, and it took a court order to require that women in Los Angeles be given patrol assignments.

CURRENT ROLE

Studies have shown that, despite being fully qualified to perform the duties of a police officer, women are still discriminated against in police work and are not expected by male officers to perform as well as "real" police officers for physical and emotional reasons. The National Center for Women and Policing has determined that a small majority of police organizations have no women in upper-level command positions and a substantial majority of have no minority women in these positions. This problem is especially severe in rural areas. In addition, studies have shown that sexual harassment is common in the police force and that the number of women entering police work is increasing at a much slower rate than previously.

BROKEN WINDOWS THEORY

The "broken windows" theory holds that social disorder breeds more disorder. The name comes from the idea that if vandals break windows on a building and those windows are not quickly repaired, the vandals will be encouraged to break more windows and other crimes in the area will increase due to the perception that rules are not being enforced. The implications of the theory for police work are that enforcement of minor crimes produces the perception of a zero-tolerance police for criminal behavior and discourages more significant criminal behavior. This theory was put into practice in New York during the 1990s, when police began acting quickly to prevent social order crimes. This is seen by some as the reason for a drop in the crime rate during that period, though this explanation is controversial.

ORDER MAINTENANCE FUNCTION OF POLICE

The order maintenance function of police emphasizes the responsibility of the police to intervene in situations where public disorder either disturbs the peace or creates conflicts that can lead to more serious crimes. Order maintenance includes such activities as breaking up arguments, arresting disruptive drunks, or asking people to turn off loud music. A problem with this order maintenance function is that laws regulating public disorder often require considerable judgment on the part of the police in their enforcement, since the line at which the law has been broken is not always clear. And there is always the possibility that police intervention in a volatile and unpredictable situation will make it even worse.

LAW ENFORCEMENT FUNCTION OF POLICE

The law enforcement function of police work involves relatively clear-cut cases of criminal activity in which the police must identify and apprehend the guilty party. Unlike the order maintenance function of the police, it is unusual for the police actually to be present at the time the law is being broken and so they must work from clues and tips. The law enforcement function requires specialized skills and often more than one type of police specialist must work on a case. Police effectiveness in this area is variable and in many cases compromised by factors beyond police control.

AGGRESSIVE PATROL

Aggressive patrol is a means of increasing the police presence in neighborhoods and giving the perception that crimes have a high likelihood of being detected and punished. Aggressive patrol strategies include sting operations, in which undercover police establish seemingly illegal operations such as gambling, fencing, and drug dealing to attract lawbreakers; raids on drug dealers; and removing firearms from the street where legally possible. Aggressive patrol is based on the "broken windows" theory of law enforcement, where preventing crime through proactive enforcement prevents crime from breeding further crime.

Modern Police Force

In addition to apprehending and tracking criminals, a typical American police force has a number of duties within the local community. Those duties may include intervening in potentially dangerous situations, such as informal street gatherings; issuing citations for traffic offenses and parking violations; directing traffic; settling domestic disputes before violence occurs; finding missing children and pets; giving directions to motorists; patrolling neighborhoods to maintain a police presence and deter criminal activity; testifying in court; protecting witnesses prior to trials; and enforcing local ordinances.

State Police Agencies

The first state police organization was the Texas Rangers, founded in 1836. Today, 49 of the 50 states have some form of state police (the exception is Hawaii), though in some states these organizations only enforce traffic laws. In others, the state police enforce the law in areas where no local police force has jurisdiction or they assist local police when needed. In a few states, including New York, Michigan, and Pennsylvania, the state police have jurisdiction throughout the state. The state police force is usually an arm of the executive branch of state government.

County Police Agencies

A county police force is usually run by the sheriff's office. The jurisdiction of the county police generally comprises those rural areas and small towns not already handled by a municipal police agency. In many states the sheriff is an elective office and the sheriff in turn appoints others, often political cronies, to positions within the local criminal justice system. Alternatively, these jobs may be filled through local civil service agencies. The size of these county police forces varies, though in some parts of the country they are quite large.

Municipal Police Agencies

A municipal police force is the police force of a city or town. These range in size from one-person police departments to the very large police forces of cities like New York and Chicago. However, the majority of these agencies employ less than 10 people. Because violent crimes are often concentrated in urban regions, these forces are likely to face more danger than state and county forces. In large metropolitan regions, there are often jurisdictional conflicts between municipal police agencies and the local agencies responsible for law enforcement in the suburbs.

Police Patrol

Patrolling the community is a primary function of a police force. Patrolling not only establishes a police presence in neighborhoods, reassuring the populace and deterring criminal activity, but allows police officers to perform certain fundamental duties. These include identifying evidence, recovering stolen property, observing and dealing with accidents or other mishaps, and enforcing traffic laws. Patrols may be motorized, they may be on foot, or they may be on horseback. Foot patrols became uncommon in the late 20th century, but have begun to reemerge in the 2000s as a means of reassuring citizens that police protection is available and to improve the quality of life for the police officers themselves.

Police Discretion

Police discretion is the ability of a police officer to choose among alternatives -- for instance, to choose which laws should be enforced, which situations require that an arrest be made, and which situations require the use of force. Because of several factors, including limited police resources , the complexity of statutory law and the variety of situations in which the law may be broken, police have to make decisions, at their discretion, as to how their job will be performed. Discretion is necessary in situations where police believe that the intent of the law (and of the legislators who passed it) does not require enforcement in all situations, where the law is antiquated and no longer appropriate for enforcement, or where the logistics of an arrest are impractical.

Pre-Arrest Investigation

Before an arrest occurs, there is generally a period during which complaints are investigated, witnesses are questioned, evidence is accumulated, and a decision is made as to whether the information so gathered warrants an arrest. Although this pre-arrest investigation generally begins after a crime is committed, in some circumstances it can begin before a crime occurs if there is sufficient evidence that a crime is going to be committed. (This is increasingly common in federal investigations.) The investigation will culminate either in an arrest or a decision that the arrest should not be made.

Arrest

An arrest, from a French word meaning "stop," is the process of taking someone into police custody so that they can be charged with a crime. It is usually preceded by an investigation and in misdemeanor cases requires an arrest warrant, unless a police officer has seen the crime in progress. (Arrests for felony offenses do not necessarily require a warrant if, according to the officer's judgment, there is rational grounds for suspicion and a reasonable certainty that the person being arrested committed the crime.) An arrest is followed by the accused being taken into police custody and booked.

Booking

Booking is the set of procedures that are taken by law enforcement officers to record the details of an accused criminal's arrest. These include recording the time and date of the arrest, the place of arrest, the name and address of the accused, and (optionally) fingerprinting and photographing of the accused. It may also include a search of the suspect's background. If the offense is minor, the accused may be given a citation and released. The details are generally recorded in some kind of police log. It is possible during the booking process for charges to be dropped by authorities (possibly due to procedural errors) and for bail to be set.

Police Department Detective Work

The role of the police department detective force (as opposed to police patrol units) is to:

1. Ascertain the identity of and apprehend criminals
2. Collect evidence in a criminal proceeding
3. Find witnesses
4. Recover stolen property

In small police departments, the patrolling officers may perform detective duties or the detective "department" may consist of a single detective. In larger departments, the detective department may be broken down into specialized squads, handling specific types of cases: homicide, burglaries, or sex crimes. Detective units may also be broken down by geographical area. Very large police departments may have detective units specializing in "bunco" (con artists) and drug crimes. Ad hoc detective units may be put together for important cases.

SWAT TEAM

A SWAT team (an acronym for Special Weapons and Tactics) is a specialized police unit that adopts military tactics and applies them to unusually dangerous situations, such as terrorist acts and hijackings. In addition to "SWAT teams," such units may be called Emergency Response Teams (ERT) or Tactical Neutralization Teams (TNT). SWAT teams can range in size from small two-person teams to forces of more than 100 officers. There is controversy surrounding the tendency of some police forces to adopt SWAT tactics and equipment for routine police community patrol work where it may not be appropriate. The first SWAT team was organized in 1964 by the Philadelphia Police Department.

SHOW UP AND LINEUP

In police terminology, a show up occurs when a crime victim is introduced one by one to a group of individuals and asked to identify which, if any, is the perpetrator. In a lineup, a victim is asked to pick the perpetrator out of an assembled group of people, often lined up in a row (hence the term "lineup"). These are considered a form of non-testimonial evidence and are acceptable to the Supreme Court as admissible evidence under some, but not all, circumstances. For instance, the police may not suggest to the victim which individual in the group they believe to be the perpetrator. The high court has also ruled that an indicted suspect has a right to have an attorney present during a lineup or show up.

STING OPERATION

A sting operation is an attempt by law enforcement officers to deceive criminals into thinking that they are taking part in an illegal enterprise or dealing with private citizens who patronize illegal enterprises when they are in fact attempting to perform illegal activities with police officers. A typical sting might consist of police officers representing narcotics purchasers in an attempt to gather evidence against drug traffickers and catch them in the act of making a drug sale. Similarly, the police may simulate a fencing operation to catch burglars trying to sell stolen merchandise. The term "sting" implies a confidence operation, albeit a legal one.

CLEARANCE RATE

The clearance rate is the percentage of crimes that result in an arrest. It is used as a yardstick in evaluating a police force or individual officers within the force. For this reason, police tend to concentrate on those crimes for which arrest is considered likely, primarily crimes in which the victim and perpetrator are acquainted, which facilitates identification of the perpetrator. These include homicide and rape. Crimes in which the perpetrator and victim are not acquainted, such as burglary and robbery, have a low clearance rate and for that reason are not always a priority among police detectives. Some crimes tend to lend themselves to the multiple-clearance method, in which solving a single crime can solve other crimes committed by the same perpetrator, which can increase clearance rates. Another easily abused method of increasing clearance rates is to define some difficult to solve crimes previously considered felonies as misdemeanors, thus increasing the clearance rate for felonies. This is called reclassification.

TRIBAL POLICE AGENCIES

Native American tribes in the United States operate under the principle of tribal sovereignty and are largely self-governing. They do not possess the total sovereignty that foreign nations have, but the tribes have a larger degree of autonomy from the federal government than do the states. As such, they have their own police forces and their own tribal criminal laws. These laws extend not only to Native Americans, but to anyone on tribal lands. The tribal police forces are supplemented by officers of the United States Bureau of Indian Affairs.

DNA FINGERPRINTING

DNA fingerprinting involves taking DNA samples from criminal suspects in the form of hair, blood, swabs of the inside of the cheek or other tissue sample and analyzing it for a distinctive signature or fingerprint that can be used to identify that specific individual's DNA. This fingerprint is unique to every person on earth (or at least the odds of two individuals producing the same signature are extremely remote, though in cases where individuals are closely related the odds are somewhat better than between two unrelated individuals). The DNA fingerprint of a crime suspect can be compared to DNA found at the scene of a crime -- for instance, using semen left by a rapist or blood left by someone injured at the crime scene. DNA evidence is generally regarded by experts as more reliable than eyewitness testimony, though there is a chance of human error in processing the DNA samples.

POLICE SCUBA UNITS

A surprising amount of police investigative work takes place underwater. Whether it involves finding a submerged body, a wrecked car, or discarded evidence, police scuba teams are an ideal way to perform this kind of investigation and are becoming increasingly common. Sometimes, as in cases involving explosives concealed underwater, the police scuba team may work in conjunction with other groups, such as US Navy divers. Police scuba diving can require a variety of skills, such as disarming bombs, navigating treacherous waters, and working in a cold environment. Scuba teams can be found in police forces both large and small.

KANSAS CITY EXPERIMENT

The Kansas City Experiment, carried out by the Kansas City, Missouri, Police Department in 1972 and 1973, attempted to gauge the effectiveness of police patrols on the public perception of police effectiveness. Three kinds of patrols were organized and carried out at various times. These were:

1. A normal patrol, with police cars cruising the streets and responding to calls;
2. A proactive patrol, in which the number of police cars was doubled or tripled during the patrol; and
3. A reactive patrol, in which there were a minimal number of police cars cruising neighborhoods and police reacted primarily to calls for assistance.

The result of the experiment was that the number of crimes and the levels of citizen satisfaction with the police were almost identical for all three types of patrols, suggesting that patrols were ineffective as a crime deterrent.

COMMUNITY POLICING

Community policing is a philosophy of police work in which police officers become part of a community, patrolling it regularly, making friends within the community, and even (in some cases) living in the community in order to strengthen the ties between the police and the communities they serve. It is believed that community policing will build trust between the police and civilians, and may give the police access to information that they would not otherwise have. Community policing is less reactive than ordinary police work and attempts to get at the roots of crime and find solutions to criminal activity within the community itself. Community policing attempts to prevent crimes by determining why they occur.

OPPORTUNISTIC THEFT BY POLICE OFFICERS

Opportunistic theft is unplanned theft that occurs when an object is left unguarded, and the thief can take it without immediate fear of consequences. Police officers sometimes engage in opportunistic theft of merchandise and money taken as evidence from criminals or found at the scene of a crime. Objects of this theft include valuables such as jewelry confiscated from a burglar, money taken from arrested suspects or even crime victims, drugs confiscated from a drug dealer, loose objects or money obtained at a crime scene, items taken from a store during a routine patrol, or even money removed from a corpse. Opportunistic theft can be considered a form of police deviance.

Police Internal Affairs Units

The internal affairs unit is that department within a law enforcement agency that investigates allegations of misconduct and lawbreaking among the law enforcement officers themselves. These investigations generally begin with the filing of a formal complaint against an officer alleging wrongdoing. These can be filed by members of the general public or by members of the police force, and can include allegations not only of police corruption but of violations of departmental policy, including sexual harassment and use of drugs. Members of an internal affairs department often find themselves separated from other police officers by the nature of their work.

Civilian Review Boards

Civilian review boards are an alternative to police internal affairs departments for investigating complaints of misconduct and lawbreaking by police officers. Many large cities have such boards. Their presence can dispel a sense on the part of the public that the police internal affairs department is unwilling to investigate complaints against officers. While these civilian boards review complaints against the police, they lack the power to discipline police officers who are found to have violated departmental regulations and can only make recommendations. Police departments often feel that the existence of civilian review boards constricts their ability to perform their work.

Legislative Control of Police Misconduct

According to some experts, a great deal of police misconduct is related to victimless crimes such as gambling, prostitution and use of illegal drugs. It has been suggested that one way to reduce police misconduct would be to eliminate the laws making these activities criminal. Some headway has been made in this direction with laws that allow gambling to occur under strict government control. Government-run lotteries are an example, as is off-track betting. However, the elimination of additional laws against victimless crimes is politically difficult and not likely to happen in the near future.

Deadly Force by Police

The use of deadly force by police -- shooting a fleeing suspect, for instance -- is a longstanding tradition in law enforcement and is generally supported by statute. Unfortunately, the limits on the use of deadly force are ill-defined by law. In general, it is expected that police will use a reasonable amount of force and no more. The Supreme Court has made some attempts to define those situations in which deadly force can be used -- for instance, in the 1985 case Tennessee v. Garner concerned itself with the right of police officers to shoot fleeing suspects under certain conditions. Some communities, particularly minority communities, worry that the police are trigger happy and will use deadly force in situations where it is not warranted, but some experts fear that police are so well-trained not to use deadly force that they will not use it when it is needed.

Case Fixing

Case fixing is a form of police corruption in which a law enforcement official has a case dropped or charges reduced against someone as a favor or in return for some form of consideration, often money. The simplest form of case fixing is bribing a police officer not to make an arrest or give out a ticket. It is frequently used to fix traffic tickets, but is often used for more serious crimes as well. It can be done by anyone in the criminal justice system who has some form of control over the process and is often done simply because someone has a friend who works on the police force or for the court.

POLICE CORRUPTION

SOCIETY AT LARGE EXPLANATION

Former Chicago police superintendent and author O.W. Wilson proposed that society itself is responsible for police corruption. He saw such corruption as the result of a slippery slope process that begins with citizens giving police officers gratuities in return for small services rendered and ends with large-scale bribery and kickbacks for a police force that has grown accustomed to receiving money from the public and no longer feels that such an arrangement is unacceptable. In other words, corruption is an outgrowth of relatively harmless interactions between the police and society at large.

STRUCTURAL EXPLANATION

Structural explanations attempt to explain crime through existing social structures. Structural theory explains police corruption as a response to the perceived conflict between the rules a police officer is expected to follow and the rule-breaking behavior exhibited by the criminal element of society with which the officer regularly deals. In addition, the officer may be exposed to older, more corrupt police officers, and their behavior may come to seem normal. Over time, the police officer may come to feel that corrupt behavior is acceptable and even expected of someone in his/her position.

ROTTEN APPLE EXPLANATION

The rotten apple explanation for police corruption assumes that corrupt behavior starts with only a few dishonest officers -- the bad apples -- and spreads from those individuals to others in the same department. The term comes from the old saying that one bad apple spoils the whole barrel. This is probably the most popular explanation for corruption among police officers themselves. It does not, however, explain the prevalence of corruption in some police departments and may well be a way in which police officers can feel better about the systems in which they work.

PLANNED THEFT BY POLICE

Unlike opportunistic theft, which is a crime committed by police officers on the spur of the moment and often without premeditation, planned theft by police represents a deliberate and sometimes systematic adoption of corrupt behavior with unquestionable criminal intent. Unlike the petty misconduct that is endemic to some police departments, planned theft is taken quite seriously by the police hierarchy and is generally dealt with in strong terms when it is detected. Planned thefts committed by police in recent years have included stopping people and taking their money, skimming money taken in drug busts, and illegal search and seizure of stolen goods. These thefts are often committed in a conspiratorial manner by multiple police officers.

SHAKEDOWN

A shakedown is an extortion scheme executed by a police officer who agrees not to report some illegal activity, often involving the breaking of an obscure law, in exchange for money. The term "shakedown" was originally a British slang term for a prostitute's bedroom, as these were once a common site for shakedown schemes. Examples would include police officers agreeing, for a price, not to enforce health code violations or to ignore gambling operations. In some cases, a shakedown can involve manufactured charges where no real crime has been committed. Shakedowns can be considered a form of police deviance.

KICKBACKS IN POLICE WORK.

Kickbacks are payments made to officials, including police, for helping to direct customers to a business enterprise. For instance, police officers can use their position of authority to refer both crime victims and criminals to attorneys, bail bondsmen, physicians, automobile repair shops, towing companies, or even funeral parlors. Kickbacks to police officers, though not uncommon, are a form of police corruption and can be considered police deviance. They are often illegal and can be looked on as a form of bribe, but can be difficult to prosecute because of the often informal nature of the kickback arrangement.

POLICE BRUTALITY

Police brutality is the excessive and unprofessional use of force by police officers. It can include verbal abuse and intimidation. It is difficult to define because police have a mandate to use force when, in their judgment, it becomes necessary. Some experts believe that it is limited to a few police officers who have a history of brutality both in their professional and personal lives that may result from a belief that they are above the law (this is known as the bad apple paradigm), but studies have shown that police brutality is relatively common in some police departments and arises from the violence inherent in the normal course of law enforcement. Cases of police brutality are often investigated by the internal affairs division of a police department, but may also become the subject of public investigations.

ESCOBEDO V. ILLINOIS

In the 1964 Supreme Court case Escobedo v. Illinois, the defendant had been denied a right to consult with an attorney by Illinois police. He was convicted on the basis of a confession made without an attorney present. The Illinois Supreme Court first overturned the conviction, then upheld it. It was finally overturned by the US Supreme Court, which upheld Escobedo's right to consult with an attorney, thereby interpreting Sixth Amendment protections as taking effect prior to the trial and even prior to the arrest. However, the Escobedo ruling did not apply these rights during the investigatory phase of the case but only to the accusatory phase.

MIRANDA V. ARIZONA

In the 1966 Supreme Court case Miranda v. Arizona, Ernesto Arturo Miranda had been convicted of rape and kidnapping on the basis of a confession made without the suspect having been informed of his right to remain silent under the law. The high court ruled that it was not sufficient that Miranda had not requested an attorney during questioning. It was necessary that he be told of his rights and then waive them. This and several other cases before the court in that session established the need for police to give a suspect what came to be known as a Miranda warning, in which the suspect is informed of his or her right to remain silent and to consult an attorney.

MIRANDA WARNING

In a Miranda warning, as established in the 1966 Supreme Court case Miranda v. Arizona, a police officer must tell a suspect the following before any questioning takes place if the evidence obtained through questioning is to be admissible in court:

1. "You have a right to remain silent."
2. "Anything you say can and will be used against you in a court of law."
3. "You have the right to consult with a lawyer and to have the lawyer present during any questioning."
4. "If you cannot afford a lawyer, one will be obtained for you if you so desire."

UNITED STATES V. WADE

In the 1967 Supreme Court case United States v. Wade, the high court dealt with the issue of an indicted suspect's right to have a lawyer present during a police lineup or show-up. In this case, the respondent had been arrested for bank robbery and placed in a police lineup where they had been identified by two bank employees. The counsel for the suspect, who had already been indicted for the crime, was present at the time. The high court held that "[t]he Sixth Amendment guarantees an accused the right to counsel not only at his trial but at any critical confrontation by the prosecution at pretrial proceedings where the results might well determine his fate and where the absence of counsel might derogate from his right to a fair trial." However, this ruling only covered suspects who had already been indicted for the crime.

DICKERSON V. UNITED STATES

In the 2000 Supreme Court case Dickerson v. United States, the high court returned to the issues adjudicated earlier in the landmark case Miranda v. Arizona (1966), where the court had ruled that police must make a suspect aware that they have the right to counsel and to remain silent under police questioning. The failure to provide this information made evidence given by the suspect in a confession inadmissible in a criminal trial. A federal statute passed in the wake of the Miranda decision had attempted to circumvent this requirement by declaring that all voluntary testimony must be considered admissible. In Dickerson, the court struck down this statute, declaring it unconstitutional.

RHODE ISLAND V. INNIS

In the 1980 Supreme Court case Rhode Island v. Innis, the high court dealt with the issue of what sort of questioning by police constituted an interrogation. At issue were the Miranda rights of a suspect who had told police, in reaction to a chance comment by an officer, where to find a weapon used in a crime. Did this chance comment by police constitute an interrogation? No, the court ruled. Miranda rights took effect "whenever a person in custody is subjected to either express questioning or its functional equivalent," but comments made by police without any expectation of a confession did not qualify as express questioning, and no Miranda rights were violated by the suspect not having a lawyer present.

UNITED STATES V. ASH

In the 1967 case United States v. Wade, the Supreme Court had determined that an indicted suspect had the right to have legal counsel present when appearing in a lineup or show-up. In the 1973 case United States v. Ash, the high court dealt with the issue of whether these same Sixth Amendment rights applied when a witness is asked to identify an indicted suspect from a lineup of photographs. The court ruled that no right to counsel exists in such a situation because it is not a "critical stage" in the pretrial process and the suspect is not even present for it.

DELAWARE V. PROUSE

In the 1979 Supreme Court case Delaware v. Prouse, the high court dealt with the constitutionality of stopping cars for random spot checks. The court ruled that there must be a reasonable cause for stopping a car; otherwise, these spot checks represent a violation of Fourth Amendment protections against unreasonable search and seizure. In this case, a police officer stopped a car and arrested its occupants when it was found that they were in possession of illicit drugs. The police officer admitted that he had had no reason for stopping that particular car, but was simply not busy at the time.

Tasers

Tasers are nonlethal devices used by police to subdue suspects. They are considered an alternative to the use of deadly force. Tasers project a probe at the suspect. The probe is connected to a wire that carries electric current into the suspect's body, causing the suspect to go into uncontrollable spasms. They have been adopted by thousands of police departments across the United States. Tasers have been praised for apparently reducing the number of shootings by those police departments that have adopted them, but their safety has not been fully studied and their use has not been standardized by uniform guidelines. Furthermore, there is evidence in some areas that the use of tasers has increased the overall use of force by police even as it has reduced the use of deadly force, prompting allegations that police have become "taser happy."

Legalization of Illicit Drugs

Some crime control arguments in favor of the legalization of illicit drugs are:

1. The prices of the drugs, which would become government regulated, would drop and users would no longer have to commit crimes in order to afford them.
2. Courts and prisons would no longer be crowded with drug-related cases, so that the criminal justice system would be free to concentrate on other crimes.
3. Organized crime would no longer profit from the sale of illicit drugs, and the violence associated with drug trafficking would disappear.
4. Government corruption associated with drug policy would be reduced.
5. The curtailment of civil liberties due to the war on drugs would stop.

Some arguments against the legalization of illicit drugs are:

1. The number of people at risk for drug abuse would increase.
2. The negative health effects caused by illicit drugs like cocaine and heroin would increase.
3. The suffering caused by extremely addictive drugs like crack cocaine would increase.
4. Many drug traffickers would have chosen a criminal career anyway, so the argument that drug legalization reduces crime is not entirely true.
5. Drug use prevents people from living productive lives.
6. Drug treatment coerced through the law enforcement system is more effective than voluntary treatment.

Preventive Control of Police Misconduct

Preventive control attempts to stop police corruption and misconduct before it can occur. It includes internal accountability, where strict guidelines are set forth stating the responsibilities of police and detail who is responsible for the conduct of specific individuals; tight supervision, which is necessary for internal accountability to be effective; and abolition of corrupting procedures. The last concerns the removal of police procedures that may encourage misconduct, such as financial obligations expected of officers (such as paying off informants) that may encourage them to find ways to pay themselves back for the loss and unrealistic levels of performance (high arrest quotas, for instance) that may necessitate violations of standard procedure.

Punitive Control of Police Misconduct

Punitive control attempts to prevent police misconduct by actively policing that conduct and disciplining officers found to have engaged in some form of police corruption. Punitive control is generally the domain of the internal affairs department of the police force. The internal affairs department usually investigates:

1. Complaints about police misconduct
2. Suspicions of misconduct
3. The death and wounding of police officers by others, including other officers
4. The death and wounding of citizens by police officers
5. The firing of weapons by officers

Internal affairs departments began to emerge in the 1940s. They are not always effective. Sometimes the internal affairs officers are themselves corrupt, or they are unwilling to expose corruption within their own police department. Furthermore, citizens are often unwilling to file complaints against the police.

Role of Police in Fighting Domestic Violence

Domestic violence, often involving wives threatened or abused physically by their husbands, is the most common reason for calls to police hotlines. However, the police have been historically reluctant to become involved in these situations for several reasons: (1) the emotional nature of domestic violence is perceived as creating a more dangerous situation than other crimes; (2) domestic violence victims will often refuse to testify; and (3) police involvement can sometimes make the situation worse. The dangerousness of these situations has been disputed, with some studies indicating that the risk to officers has been exaggerated. The women's movement has encouraged more police involvement in domestic disputes, and there are indications that jailing a spouse for a short time lessens the possibility of violence.

Chimel v. California

In the 1969 Supreme Court case Chimel v. California, the high court dealt with the issue of how extensive police searches may be during an arrest. In this case, police had gone to the home of a robbery suspect, Chimel, arriving before the suspect came home. When the suspect arrived, he was informed that the police were going to search his home without a warrant "on the basis of the lawful arrest." The search, which took nearly two hours and covered the entire house and its garage, turned up several items of evidence used to convict the accused. Chimel appealed the case, alleging that his Fourth Amendment guarantee against unreasonable search and seizure had been violated. The court agreed and specified that a reasonable warrantless search should include only the area under the immediate control of the suspect, to guarantee that it is free of weapons or evidence that might be destroyed.

Florida v. Bostick

In the 1991 Supreme Court case Florida v. Bostick, the high court dealt with the issue of consensual searches of bus passengers. A consensual search is a search performed with the consent of the individual. At issue was the question of whether a passenger on the bus could reasonably feel free to decline the search. The court ruled that the warrantless search of a bus passenger violated Fourth Amendment protections against unreasonable search and seizure because such a search "exhibit[s] all of the elements of coercion associated with a typical bus sweep." In other words, the search is coerced rather than consensual.

Illinois v. Wardlow

In the 2000 Supreme Court case Illinois v. Wardlow, the high court considered the issue of when police have a sufficiently reasonable suspicion to justify a warrantless search of an individual. The defendant, William Wardlow, had been searched by police who had seen him acting in a manner that suggested he was trying to flee from them. Wardlow argued that this violated his Fourth Amendment protections against unreasonable search and seizure, and that the gun they had taken from him should not have been admissible as evidence at his trial. Although Wardlow claimed that there could have been many reasons that a person would seem to be fleeing police, the high court upheld his conviction and deemed the suspicions of the officers to have been a reasonable basis for the search.

Indianapolis v. Edmond

In the 2000 Supreme Court case Indianapolis v. Edmond, the court considered the circumstances under which law enforcement officers can perform searches without a reasonable suspicion of wrongdoing. At issue were police roadblocks and the use of trained dogs to detect illegal drugs. The right of the police to conduct roadblocks had already been established, but the court had specified that searches performed as a result of these roadblocks must "serve special needs, beyond the normal need for law enforcement." In this case, the court found that a "general interest in crime control" in lieu of a specific target or rationale for the search was not sufficient to justify such roadblocks.

Tennessee v. Garner

In the 1985 Supreme Court case Tennessee v. Garner, the high court dealt with the issue of the use of deadly force by police officers to stop a fleeing criminal. A suspect, Garner, had been shot and killed by a Memphis policeman, and the victim's father had sued authorities. A local court had ruled that the shooting was authorized by statute. However, an appeals court reversed the decision, holding that shooting a suspect is a form of "seizure" and is unconstitutional under the Fourth Amendment. The Supreme Court agreed, ruling that such a shooting represented a reasonable search and seizure only if it is "necessary to prevent the escape and the officer has probable cause to believe that the suspect poses a significant threat of death or serious physical injury to the officer or others."

Terry v. Ohio

In the 1968 Supreme Court case Terry v. Ohio, a police officer had performed a "pat down" search of a man he suspected was about to commit a robbery. With the gun as evidence, he arrested the man and his companion. The two men were convicted on the basis of the evidence. The conviction was appealed on the grounds that the pat down search and the police officer's taking of the gun had constituted illegal search and seizure, and was thus a violation of the Eighth Amendment. The court ruled that such a search for concealed weapons based on the reasonable suspicion that an individual is about to commit a crime (or is leaving the scene of one) is constitutional.

Arrest

The steps that lead to an arrest are:

1. Detection -- Police become aware that a crime has been committed. Usually, this is because of a report of the crime has been called in on the police hotline or a security alarm has been triggered.
2. Preliminary investigation -- The crucial stage during which the first officer on the screen gathers facts, interviews the victim, and apprehends a suspect if present. The crime scene is secured and further investigation is requested.
3. Follow-up investigation -- A detailed investigation, often by a team of specialized experts, and the analysis of the data acquired to determine what is known and what can be done.

4. Clearance and arrest -- When enough information has been acquired and analyzed to support a decision to arrest a suspect, the crime is said to be "cleared." The arrest is then made.

Line and Staff Functions

Line functions in a police force are those operations performed in the field while staff functions are the clerical and administrative operations that support this work. The field officers who patrol the streets, investigate crime scenes, direct traffic, etc., are doing essential crime solving and order maintenance tasks, making these the most visible aspects of police work. (They are, in effect, the front line of police work.) But the administrative operations performed out of the view of most of the public are equally essential, though the majority of police employees are involved in line functions of one kind or another.

Incident-Driven Policing

Incident-driven policing is a reactive police strategy driven by calls from the public reporting problems that the police are expected to solve. About a third of these tend to be crimes. The rest involve some sort of order maintenance (asking a neighbor to turn down a loud stereo, breaking up a rowdy crowd) or service. While proactive strategies (such as raids and stings) are used by police forces, the majority of police work is incident driven. This is in part because public reaction to proactive police work can be negative, in that it gives the perception that the police are interfering in people's private lives, something that is largely regarded as inappropriate in a democratic society.

Police Personality

There is no single personality type that can be attributed to all persons who work in law enforcement. Nonetheless, there are certain characteristics that are common in the profession. These characteristics are apparently acquired through the nature of the work. These include suspiciousness, which results from the need to be alert to covert criminal activity, and cynicism, which comes in large part from frequent exposure to the more deviant aspects of human nature. There is also a sense among some police officers that they are isolated from the rest of society, in part because of the negative reaction of others to the police officer's role of enforcing laws that may not be popular. Female police officers are confident and independent to a greater degree than women outside the police force.

Stress in Police Work

Law enforcement is a stressful profession and the stress can arise from several different factors. Obviously, the generally dangerous nature of the work leads to stress, but this external stress is only one reason for the stressful nature of the profession; other sources of stress include the bureaucratic, rigorous, paramilitary nature of the work itself (organizational stress), the exposure to deviant behavior and a sometimes hostile public (operational stress), and emotional strain between the police officers and their own families, friends and coworkers (personal stress). This stress increases the sense of isolation already felt by many in the profession.

Police Training

In most jurisdictions, police candidates are required to participate in basic training programs. This training can take place at a police academy or can be part of a commercially available course for which the candidate must pay tuition. The training concerns the mechanics of the job, such as how to use weapons, and includes legal training. Some of these courses are offered by local community colleges. Once hired, officers go through a probationary period where they learn necessary skills from other, more experienced officers and from their own experiences on the street.

Minorities in Police Work

For most of their history, American police forces have been dominated by white males. This began to change about 40 years ago. The Equal Employment Opportunity Act of 1972 required governments on both the state and local levels to hire qualified minorities for all positions and police forces began making an effort to recruit African-Americans, Hispanics, Asians and members of other minorities for police work. Women also began to enter the police force. Today, African-Americans represent 10 percent of the police force nationally and women represent 5 percent. Approximately 7 percent of the police force is now Hispanic. The addition of minorities to the police force has helped to defuse some but not all of the tension that exists between the police and minority communities.

Court System

HISTORICAL ROLE OF COURTS IN AMERICAN LIFE

Courts have traditionally been not only the place where adjudication -- the determination of the guilt of an accused suspect -- occurs but have occupied a central place in American life. The buildings have literally been the center, geographically, of many towns and occupy a prominent place in city centers. They are a place where civil as well as criminal justice is meted out and civil marriage ceremonies are performed. Over the years, a number of different types of courts have evolved, including mayor's courts, night courts, probate courts, and supreme courts, each with its own special purpose within the system. Circuit courts evolved to provide justice over large regions where only smaller courts would have been previously available.

DUAL COURT SYSTEM OF THE UNITED STATES

There are two different kinds of court in the United States, federal courts and state courts. The state courts are organized differently in every state, according to local statute. The US Court system is unified by federal statute. In each system there is a hierarchy of courts, at the top of which is a supreme court. (Similarly, there is a hierarchy of supreme courts, with the United States Supreme Court representing the court of highest appeal.) Different courts in the system have different jurisdictions, with courts of general jurisdiction and courts of limited jurisdiction. Although there is some overlap between the cases heard in the two court systems, federal courts generally deal with violations of federal law and situations that affect the United States as a whole. There is considerable variation in the way laws are interpreted in different courts of the state system, in part because of regional differences in attitude.

FEDERAL BUREAU OF PRISONS AND THE FEDERAL PRISON SYSTEM

The Federal Bureau of Prisons (BOP) operates all federal prisons in the United States. It is a division of the United States Department of Justice, established in 1930. The prisons that it maintains house approximately 150,000 inmates. More than half of that population has been convicted of drug-related offenses. Relatively few inmates of these federal prisons are violent offenders; these tend to be mainly in state prisons. On the other hand, federal prisons tend to house more prisoners convicted of white collar crimes and bank robbery. The federal prison system includes prisons for women and for underage offenders.

COURT OF GENERAL JURISDICTION AND COURT OF LIMITED JURISDICTION

A court of general jurisdiction is a court that is authorized to hear all kinds of cases, including criminal cases, civil cases, juvenile cases, probate cases, and so forth. These cases may be based on violations of civil law or of constitutional law. There are more than 3,000 courts of general jurisdiction in the United States. Some of these cases may have been referred from lower courts. A court of limited jurisdiction is confined to hearing only cases of a certain kind. All federal courts in the US are courts of limited jurisdiction.

JUDICIAL CIRCUIT

A judicial circuit is a grouping of courts in several districts, usually counties, presided over by a single judge or group of judges. These judges move from one circuit court to the next, presiding over cases in each. This process is known as "riding the circuit," a term that originated at a time when judges would go from court to court on horseback. Such judges are called circuit court judges. A circuit court is usually a local county court during periods when the circuit court judge is not present. These county courts are part of the state's system of lower courts when not being used as circuit courts.

APPELLATE COURT

An appellate court, or appeals court, is a court that hears cases that are being appealed after first being heard at a lower court. (An appeal is a judgment of a lower court being reviewed by a higher court.) Such a court is said to have appellate jurisdiction. Generally, appellate courts determine whether due process was correctly followed by the lower court rather than reviewing the evidence and determining the facts. These appeals can involve both civil and criminal cases. These courts are required to hear cases if they have been appealed according to the proper rules. However, to reduce the case load at appellate courts, an intermediate court of appeals may review cases before they reach the higher courts.

US DISTRICT COURTS

The US District Courts were created in 1789 by the Judiciary Act. At the time, a District Court was established in each of the 13 states, though the number of District Courts has subsequently grown to 94, including courts in the District of Columbia and several US territories (Puerto Rico, the Virgin Islands, Guam, and the Northern Mariana Islands). These are courts that hear matters of national importance and even of national security, including cases involving treason, espionage, jurisdictional disputes and copyright violation. These can be criminal cases or civil cases.

LOWER COURT JUDGE

Judges have ultimate authority over what happens in the courtroom. They serve as arbiters and administrators. Among their responsibilities are:

- Guaranteeing that due process is followed and that the rights of the defendant are upheld;
- Guaranteeing that both the public and justice are served;
- Overseeing the appointment and duties of court personnel and monitoring budgetary and record-keeping matters.

The specific duties of a judge will vary depending on what type of court he/she presides over, with judges in smaller, local courts taking on more administrative duties than judges in larger systems.

GRAND JURY

A grand jury examines the evidence in a case and determines whether there is probable cause for prosecution. It consists of between 12 to 23 private citizens. The US Constitution requires that grand juries be used in federal trials for "capital and infamous crimes," but the Supreme Court has held that their use in state trials is optional. There are two types of grand jury: the investigatory grand jury (which examines general evidence of criminal activity to determine whether anyone should be prosecuted) and the accusatory grand jury (which reviews the evidence against those already charged and determines whether it is sufficient for prosecution). The latter is more common and is generally empanelled for a set period of time, often three months. The grand jury produces either a true bill, which states that the evidence is sufficient for prosecution, or a no bill, which states that the evidence is insufficient for prosecution. A true bill results in an indictment.

UNITED STATES SUPREME COURT

The US Supreme Court was established under Article 3 of the United States Constitution, which reads "[t]he judicial Power of the United States, shall be vested in one supreme Court, and in such inferior Courts as the Congress may from time to time ordain and establish." Although allowed for in the Constitution, the Supreme Court was actually created by the Judiciary Act of 1789, which set the number of Supreme Court justices at six. (The number is now nine.) Under the act, the Supreme Court became the court of appeals for cases heard by federal courts and at times for cases heard by state courts.

The US Supreme Court is the highest court in the country. It is the court of appeals for other federal courts and is sometimes called the court of last resort because no more appeals are possible after a Supreme Court decision has been made, even if it's a decision not to hear the case. The Supreme Court is authorized by Article III of the United States Constitution and was officially established, under President George Washington, by the Judiciary Act of 1789. It is presided over by nine justices, one of whom holds the title of Chief Justice of the United States. These positions carry lifetime tenure, though it is possible for a Supreme Court justice to be impeached. The justices are nominated by the President of the United States and confirmed by the US Senate.

Jurisdictional Scope

The primary, but not sole, function of the US Supreme Court is to assure that federal and local laws are in accordance with the US Constitution and that due process has been followed by the lower courts. However, the Constitution extends the court's mandate to include "all Cases affecting Ambassadors, other public Ministers and Consuls; to all Cases of admiralty and maritime Jurisdiction; to Controversies to which the United States shall be a Party; to Controversies between two or more States; between a State and Citizens of another State; between Citizens of different States; between Citizens of the same State claiming Lands under Grants of different States, and between a State, or the Citizens thereof, and foreign States, Citizens or Subjects."

Rule of Four

When a writ of certiorari is received by the Supreme Court requesting that they review a case from a lower court, at least four of the justices must agree to hear the case before the high court reviews it. This is called the Rule of Four. This is slightly less than a majority of the court and is intended to prevent the majority from controlling which cases are heard. The rule of four is not mandated by the Constitution or by statute, but is a tradition that has evolved within the Court itself and was first adopted in the late 19th century.

Affirming, Reversing, and Remanding

When the Supreme Court hears a case from the lower courts, it has these options:

- Affirming the decision -- Upholding the decision of the lower court, a decision that means the Court feels there are no reversible errors in the case.
- Reversing and remanding the decision -- Declaring that there are judicial errors in the lower court decision and returning the case to the original court so that a new decision may be rendered. This does not mean that the defendant in the case is free or blameless. However, the prosecutors may decide that there is no point in retrying the case, because in many instances the original evidence used to convict has been declared "tainted." In other cases, the Supreme Court decision may require moving the trial to a less prejudicial venue or a change of the punishment imposed in the lower court.

Missouri Plan

The Missouri Plan, which is advocated by the American Bar Association, is a system for appointing, electing and rejecting judges. Under it, a judge is appointed by the governor based on a list of candidates supplied by attorneys, citizens and a currently sitting judge. After a fixed term the judge's appointment is put up for public vote and voters may choose to reelect or reject the judge. If the judge is rejected, a new judge is appointed through the same procedure. The Missouri Plan (also called the Merit Plan) combines the appointment of judges with the election of judges. It is currently used in several states.

COURT CLERK

The court clerk calls cases before the judge, keeps the court's records, collects fines, and ensures the security of the evidence to be presented at a trial. In some jurisdictions, court clerks may preside over marriage ceremonies or prepare formal writs. In some instances, judges may play the role of court clerk if no other clerk is available or the duties of the clerk may be spread out over several assistant clerks. In large court systems, the clerk can be a powerful figure and the job is considered part of the career path that young attorneys can take if they want to work in the prosecutor's office.

COURT REPORTER/COURT STENOGRAPHER

The court reporter, also called the court stenographer, reports on (and often keeps the official record of) court proceedings. At one time court records were kept in shorthand, an art that has now almost entirely disappeared. Modern court reporters work with stenographic machines that place text on moving tapes or cassettes in such a way that they can later be read mechanically and transferred to the court file-keeping system. Attempts to replace court reporters with machines have largely failed, in part because one of the duties of the court reporter is to point out when testimony is unclear or inaudible, a job that is difficult to automate. Nonetheless, modern court reporters do their job with considerable assistance from computers.

BAILIFF

The bailiff, or sheriff, is a security officer of the court. The role is often taken by a deputy or marshal. The job of the bailiff is to announce the arrival of the judge and maintain discipline in the courtroom. In some instances, the job extends to keeping track of various attorneys and witnesses, as well as giving directions and information to the defendants. A bailiff is generally empowered to make arrests and serve as a police officer within the courthouse, but not necessarily out of it. The concept of the bailiff originated in medieval Europe.

US COURTS OF APPEAL

There are 13 United States Courts of Appeal. They hear cases appealed from the US District Courts as well as from certain other courts that rule on specialized matters, such as international trade. Each of the 13 courts represents a circuit covering a geographic region, with all 13 courts collectively covering the US states and territories, and the District of Columbia. For instance, the United States Court of Appeals for the Third Circuit has jurisdiction over cases appealed from the district courts for Delaware, New Jersey, Pennsylvania, and the Virgin Islands. Not all cases from the lower court are appealed to the Courts of Appeal. Certain kinds of cases can go directly to the Supreme Court.

WRIT OF CERTIORARI

A writ of certiorari, from a Latin term meaning "to be more fully informed," is a writ requesting judicial review of a case. It is generally filed by the Supreme Court to a lower court, asking to review a case decided by that court for which no appeal would otherwise be available. The writ is issued if four or more Supreme Court justices believe that there is reason to review the case and is usually a response to a petition for a writ of certiorari filed by a petitioner. A denial of the writ of certiorari by the high court does not mean that the court approves of the lower court decision, but simply that they are not going to hear the case.

Justice of the Peace

A justice of the peace is a court official with many, but not necessarily all, of the powers of a judge. Justices of the peace are common in small, often rural, districts. The purview of a justice of the peace varies according to local statute, but often involves only misdemeanors and certain civil proceedings such as marriages. The justice of the peace is usually an elected official rather than an appointed one. In many jurisdictions, the functions of the justice of the peace have been replaced by a magistrate court.

Immunity from Prosecution

Immunity from prosecution is a waiver of prosecution granted to a person, often a witness in a criminal case, in return for some service. For instance, a witness who feels that their testimony in a trial may be self-incriminating and would normally invoke Fifth Amendment rights against self-incrimination may be granted immunity in return for testifying. There are two types of immunity. The first is transactional immunity, sometimes known as "blanket immunity," which grants total immunity from criminal prosecution for the crimes in question, even in future trials. The second is use immunity, which grants immunity from prosecution resulting from the testimony, but not necessarily from future prosecution, for the crimes.

Contempt Power of the Grand Jury

Grand juries, because they are able to subpoena witnesses, are granted the ability to find those witnesses in contempt of court if they do not comply. Those found in contempt are subject to imprisonment. There are some who believe this power can be used and abused for unconstitutional purposes. For instance, journalists compelled to testify before a grand jury about their sources of information have been imprisoned for refusal to testify. This refusal is generally predicated on the grounds that such testimony is in violation of First Amendment guarantees of freedom of the press.

Indictment, Information and Presentment

An indictment is a document produced by a grand jury charging a suspect with a crime. A presentment is also a document filed by a grand jury and is similar to an indictment, listing the evidence meriting prosecution in a criminal trial, but it is returned by an investigatory grand jury rather than an accusatory grand jury. An information is a document that in some jurisdictions is filed by a prosecutor, formally accusing a suspect of a crime and providing a full list of the charges, evidence, and specific accusations being made. Having an information filed by a prosecutor is an alternative to having a grand jury produce an indictment.

Nolle Prosequi

Nolle prosequi, from a Latin term meaning "unwilling to pursue," is a declaration that the prosecution in a criminal case no longer wishes to prosecute the case. It is a discretionary ability given prosecutors that allows them to drop a case already begun if they feel that the evidence is either insufficient or inadmissible, or if they have negotiated a new plea bargain. While considered controversial because of the potential it offers for corruption or favoritism on the part of a prosecutor, it is considered a valid prosecutorial power and has been upheld by appellate courts.

Plea

Role of Prosecutors

The prosecutor controls the plea bargain, which is essentially an agreement between the prosecution and the attorney for the defendant. All other participants hold subsidiary roles. The prosecutor chooses what concessions should be made to the defendant, and what the state will get in return. Guidelines may be available in some jurisdictions specifying what the prosecutor can do in a plea bargain, but generally this is left to the prosecutor's judgment. The prosecutor must take a number of factors into account in a plea bargain, including the seriousness of the case, the court caseload, the strength of the case, and the attitude of the judge.

ROLE OF THE DEFENSE COUNSEL AND THE DEFENDANT

The defense attorney, as the representative for the defendant, has the second most important role in a plea bargain. The defense attorney bargains directly with the prosecutor and conveys the terms of the bargain to the defendant. The defense attorney must explain the bargain and the various alternatives to the client and give advice on those alternatives. It is the responsibility of the defense attorney to make sure that the defendant is aware of everything that goes on during the plea bargain. Thus, the defense attorney is a mediator between the defendant and client. The defendant has very little to do with the process, though they hold the ultimate decision as to whether or not the plea bargain is acceptable. They may also be called upon to provide information for the prosecutor.

ROLE OF THE JUDGE AND THE VICTIM

Federal judges may not participate in a plea bargain, according to federal statute. State judges may or may not participate, depending on the jurisdiction. When the judge does participate, his or her role is largely advisory and assures fairness and consistency in the process. The role of judges in a plea bargain is controversial, because it lessens the judge's objectivity (or the appearance of objectivity) in accepting the plea after bargaining is complete. The victim is generally given some say in the plea bargain, but this may consist of no more than making the victim aware that negotiations are taking place. In a very few jurisdictions, the victim can be present during the negotiations, or their opinions on the plea bargain may be entered into the public record.

DEFENSE ATTORNEY

A defense attorney's role in a case begins at the moment when the defendant is arrested and can continue after the trial if appeals are filed. The defense attorney can provide advice to a defendant newly accused of a crime; can help investigate the case to learn the facts; can determine what the evidence against the client is based on interviews with the prosecution, witnesses, and police; can appear at bail hearings and participate in plea negotiations; filing pre-trial motions; helping select the jury; representing the defendant during the trial itself; finding a basis for appeal (if any); and presenting the case for an appeal to the appellate court.

PARENS PATRIAE

Parens patriae is a Latin term meaning the "parent state" or the "state as parent." In law, it refers to the ability of the state to become the guardian of a child being abused or neglected by his or her rightful parents. In criminal law, the concept of parens patriae has been extended to allow the case to intervene in the care of a child who has violated the law on the theory that the child's behavior is somehow the fault of the parent. The concept of parens patriae as interpreted by prison reformers led to the establishment of the juvenile court system. The first such system was established in 1899 by the Illinois Juvenile Court Act.

IN LOCO PARENTIS

In loco parentis is a Latin term meaning "in the place of parents." It refers to the role of organizations such as schools that assume responsibility for individuals who, because of their youth, would normally still be the responsibility of their parents. Under the doctrine of in loco parentis these organizations assume much of the role of parent, a role that sometimes conflicts with the rights of students as interpreted by the court. The Supreme Court has increasingly granted due process rights to students in disciplinary proceedings, despite the in loco parentis status of the schools themselves.

JUVENILE COURT SYSTEM

The juvenile court system began as an effort by reformers to protect children. This movement was known as the "child savers". Its supporters believed that children should not be held accountable for their actions in the same way as adults, and that rehabilitation of young offenders was a less difficult task and should be handled differently than the rehabilitation of adults. The first juvenile court was established in Chicago in 1899, and by 1945, there juvenile courts existed across the United States. Juvenile courts handle cases involving those who were a certain age (usually 18 but in some cases the age is lower) at the time the violation was committed. Criminal violations by a juvenile are referred to as delinquency and the offender as a delinquent. In addition to these criminal violations, juveniles may be tried for status offenses. Juvenile courts can also determine the status of abused and neglected children.

JUVENILE JUSTICE SYSTEM

PETITION

A juvenile petition is used instead as an arrest warrant when an underage individual has committed an act considered either delinquency (an act that would be considered a crime if committed by an adult) or a status offense (an act that is only considered a crime because it is committed by a child). The petition, which can be filed not only by police, but by private individuals such as parents, describes the alleged offense and begins the criminal justice process. Once the petition has been filed, the juvenile offender must appear at an intake hearing.

INTAKE HEARING

An intake hearing is the next step in the juvenile justice process after a juvenile petition has been filed. It is a judicial process that does not involve a judge and is not held in a standard courtroom. It is presided over by the intake officer or hearing officer, who has been assigned by the juvenile court to review the facts of the case and possibly discuss the matter with the police and the offender's parents. The intake officer has the power to dismiss the case without further action, but may also make a decision in the case or even pass it on to a judge for trial in a juvenile court.

DETENTION HEARING

The detention hearing is, in most jurisdictions, the next step in the juvenile justice process after the intake hearing. Its purpose is to decide whether a juvenile offender is to be held in custody by the state or released to a parent or guardian. A number of factors are taken into account in making this decision: Is the child a threat to the community? Is the child in danger of abuse from parents? The well-being of the child should be of as much importance here as the safety of the community. This decision may also involve psychological screening of the juvenile offender to determine if emotional problems are involved. Ideally, if the offender is to be detained, it will be in a special facility for juveniles, but in many cases adult facilities are used.

ADJUDICATION INQUIRY

The adjudication inquiry is the next step in the juvenile justice system after the detention hearing. It is a closed hearing in front of a judge and is similar in purpose to the intake hearing. The judge may decide to dismiss the case at this point or pass it on for a formal adjudication hearing. The adjudication hearing is not always used. In some jurisdictions, the juvenile offender may have the alternative of counseling. However, it is within the power of the offender or the offender's parents to request a formal hearing if one is desired.

Adjudication Hearing

The adjudication hearing is the next step in the juvenile justice system after the adjudication inquiry. It is not a criminal trial and is classified as a civil proceeding, but it bears certain similarities to a trial. It is presided over by a judge who is to decide whether the juvenile offender has committed the offense specified in the petition. The judge acts on behalf of the underage offender and not only determines whether the offense was committed, but whether the child's home life is adequate. The judge can choose to dismiss the case or schedule a disposition hearing.

Disposition Hearing

The disposition hearing is the next step in the juvenile justice process after the adjudication hearing. It is also the final step in the process. The judge hears the case and, if he or she does not dismiss it, can place the juvenile offender on probation, can order the offender into an institution, can require community service, or can even order the child removed from his or her home and placed in foster care. In many cases, either a fine or some form of restitution program is required. If the juvenile offender is placed on probation, an officer of the court is assigned to supervise him/her.

Juvenile Justice Process

Although the precise steps may vary by jurisdiction and the case may be dismissed before all steps are complete, the juvenile justice process generally proceeds as follows:

- A petition is filed stating the details of the offense.
- An intake hearing is held to determine if the case should be further processed.
- A detention hearing is held to determine whether the child shall remain in custody or released to the parents.
- An adjudication inquiry is held by a judge who may order a formal adjudication hearing.
- A disposition hearing is held to decide whether the child will be placed in an institution, foster care, made to pay restitution, or other rehabilitative or protective requirement.

Waiver of Jurisdiction

A waiver of jurisdiction is used to move a case from juvenile court to adult court. In other words, it determines whether an underage offender is to be treated as an adult rather than a juvenile, allowing them to be subjected to the same treatment and punishment as an adult offender. Local statutes allow a waiver of jurisdiction for offenders over a certain age or for those who have committed certain crimes. For instance, it is possible in some states for offenders under the age of 10, or young offenders who have committed murder, to be tried as an adult. The Supreme Court set down rules for the granting of a waiver of jurisdiction in the 1966 Kent v. United States.

Kent v. United States

In the 1966 Supreme Court case Kent v. United States, the high court set down specific rules in an attempt to make the granting of a waiver of jurisdiction (where a juvenile case is transferred to adult court) less arbitrary. The court determined that there must be a waiver hearing before the waiver can be granted, and most rules of due process apply at this hearing. In its decision, the court wrote that "[t]he parens patriae philosophy of the Juvenile Court 'is not an invitation to procedural arbitrariness'" and thus held juvenile courts to a higher standard than previously occurred. The case in question was remanded to a District Court for a decision as to whether the waiver of jurisdiction was reasonable and ordered that the conviction be voided if it was not, since the offender was now too old to be retried in juvenile court.

In re Gault

In re Gault was a 1967 Supreme Court case that established the applicability of due process in juvenile justice cases. The case involved a 15-year-old offender accused of making obscene phone calls. He was placed in custody without explanation or being informed of his right to counsel. At the trial hearsay testimony was allowed and no transcript was kept. The high court determined in an 8-to-1 decision that Gault's Fourteenth Amendment rights to due process had been violated, fully establishing for the first time that due process applied to juvenile as well as adult cases. Prior to Gault, due process was routinely denied in most juvenile cases.

In re Winship, Breed v. Jones, and McKeiver v. Pennsylvania

These were landmark Supreme Court cases involving the rights of juvenile offenders.

- In re Winship -- In this case, the court determined that the standard of "beyond a reasonable doubt" applied in juvenile cases.
- Breed v. Jones -- In this case, the court extended protection against double jeopardy (being tried twice for the same crime) to juvenile offenders.
- McKeiver v. Pennsylvania -- In this case, the court declared that while juvenile offenders could be tried by jury, they did not automatically have the right to a jury trial and such a trial could be denied at the discretion of the judge.

New Jersey v. T.L.O.

In the 1985 Supreme Court case New Jersey v. T.L.O., the high court dealt with the issue of whether evidence obtained by a school in searching a student's property is unconstitutional under Fourth Amendment protections against illegal search and seizure. The central questions in this case were whether the individual performing the search could be considered a private individual (in which case the search was legal) or a government agent (in which case the search would be unconstitutional), whether the school was acting in loco parentis (a Latin term meaning "in the place of parents") and whether the search could be considered reasonable. The case involved marijuana and drug paraphernalia seized from a student's purse. The court determined that this was a violation of the student's Fourth Amendment rights, and that students have an expectation of privacy.

Initial Appearance

The initial appearance is the first appearance of the accused before a judge and is intended to fulfill due process requirements that the accused be formally apprised of charges within a reasonable amount of time after the arrest. At the initial appearance bail can be set, if it was not set during the booking. The defendant may be released on his/her own recognizance during this phase. For minor offenses, the entire trial may be completed during the initial appearance and the defendant sentenced, or the judge, upon determining that there is insufficient evidence to support the charges, may dismiss the case.

Preliminary Hearing

A preliminary hearing is used to reduce overloaded courtroom schedules and protect defendants against unnecessary prosecution. They are not common. At a preliminary hearing, a judge can hear the evidence to determine whether there is probable cause to believe that the accused is guilty, whether due process has been followed during the arrest and booking of the accused, whether evidence has been obtained in a legal and reasonable manner, and whether the case deserves further attention by the authorities. Bail may be set during a preliminary hearing if it has not been set in an earlier stage of the process. Preliminary hearings may be waived if it is believed that they will cause testimony to be entered prematurely into the public record and damage the reputation of the accused.

Arraignment

Arraignment is the beginning of the trial process, during which the defendant is presented with a formal accusation and during which the defendant may enter a plea. That plea will usually be guilty, not guilty, or nolo contendere ("no contest"). Nolo contendere is roughly equivalent to a guilty plea, but does not connote any admission of guilt, a fact that could be admitted as evidence in future court proceedings against the defendant. If the defendant pleads guilty, the court must determine that this plea was made without coercion. If the defendant pleads not guilty, it must be determined if they are mentally competent and have a lawyer. If the defendant makes no plea at all they are said to be "standing mute," which is considered equivalent to a plea of "not guilty."

Trial Process

The trial process is the most complicated and potentially time-consuming portion of the criminal justice process. It consists of a number of steps in this order: Defense and prosecuting attorneys make pre-trial motions, if any, for reasons such as suppressing evidence and postponing the trial. Once this phase ends, the trial proper begins, with opening statements by the defense and prosecuting attorneys. The prosecution then presents its case, followed by a presentation of the defense's case. The prosecution is given a chance for rebuttal, as is the defense. Finally, each side makes its closing statements. If it's a jury trial, the jury is charged with returning a verdict. The jury or the judge then announces the verdict and, if the defendant is found guilty, the defense is given an opportunity to file post-trial motions (for instance, to have the jury set aside). If the defendant is found not guilty, this is the end of the criminal justice process. If the defendant is found guilty, the judge pronounces sentence.

Sentencing Process

Sentencing is the final function performed by a judge in the criminal justice process. The sentencing process may involve a pre-sentence investigation, or PSI, where the defendant's past is investigated to see if there are extenuating circumstances that would either reduce or increase the severity of a sentence. The judge then uses the relevant sentencing guidelines for the jurisdiction to set a prison sentence or alternative punishment, including fines, probation, community service, or even the death penalty. A prison may involve a range of years (10-30, for instance), with a parole board later determining how much of the sentence must be served.

Appeals Process

The appeals process can begin as soon as sentencing is complete and, in some cases, can continue as long as the appellee (convicted person making the appeal) remains in prison or even after. An appeal is an attempt to change the judge's decision and is based on claims that due process was not properly followed during the criminal justice process, that the sentence is unfair, or that new evidence has emerged. Appeals are initially brought before an appellate court, which must consider all appeals brought before it. If a lower court refuses to grant the appeal, it can be taken to a higher court, in some cases all the way to the United States Supreme Court.

Opening Statements

The opening statements in a trial allow the prosecution and defense, in that order, to summarize their cases before the jury. These do not need to be detailed descriptions of the crime or the evidence that will follow. In fact, the defense attorney is not required to make an opening statement at all and can simply wait for the jury to be exposed to the evidence presented during the rest of the trial. (The prosecution, however, always makes an opening statement.) It is also not uncommon for both sides to use the opening statement as a chance to win the jury's support from the very beginning, though this can backfire if unexpected evidence emerges during the trial and contradicts the opening statement.

WITNESS

Three categories of witness are listed and described below:

1. Lay witness -- Someone with personal knowledge of the crime. The lay witness's knowledge cannot be based on conjecture or hearsay.
2. Police witness -- A police officer with knowledge of the case. In many cases this is the arresting officer or some officer who was present at the time of the arrest. A police witness may attest to details of the crime that they personally have witnessed or to details of the pre-arrest investigation.
3. Expert witness -- Someone with expertise in a technical area relevant to the crime. Examples include experts on DNA evidence or on the psychological state of the defendant. Expert witnesses are controversial inasmuch as they amount to paid testimony, with expert witnesses willing to testify to almost any theory deemed beneficial to either the prosecution or the defense.

CORONER

The job of the coroner is to determine the cause of suspicious or violent deaths. The coroner is an official, generally in the employ of a county, who has been appointed or elected to the position. The coroner works with a number of assistants who have expertise in various forms of medical evidence. Because a coroner is either an elected or appointed position, political skills are more important in obtaining the position than medical expertise. For that reason, coroners tend to have little or no medical background. In many jurisdictions, coroners have been dispensed with altogether and replaced by medical examiners, a role generally taken by a licensed physician.

BEYOND A REASONABLE DOUBT

In finding the defendant guilty in a criminal trial, the jury is told that it must do so "beyond a reasonable doubt." This means that jurors must not act on a hunch or some intuitive feeling that the defendant is guilty, but at the same time do not need to banish all doubt about that guilt from their minds. Reasonable doubt is doubt about the defendant's guilt that remains even after a fair and sensible appraisal of the evidence presented during the trial by the prosecution and the defense.

EVIDENCE

The four major types of evidence used in trials are:

- Real evidence -- objects or photographs that represent physical evidence of how the crime occurred. These can include fingerprints, murder weapons, photographs of wounds or photographs of the crime scene itself;
- Testimonial evidence -- statements by witnesses about the crime or the real evidence;
- Direct evidence -- testimony by eyewitnesses to the crime itself;
- Circumstantial evidence -- evidence that indirectly implies facts about the crime.

These are not mutually exclusive types. Some evidence may fall into more than one category.

SEQUESTRATION OF A JURY

A jury is said to be sequestered when the jury members must remain isolated from contact with the outside world even when court is not in session -- in the evenings or on weekends, for instance.

This is usually done in high-profile cases where public interest is so high and the proceedings so well publicized that there is a high likelihood of jurors becoming prejudiced through information obtained outside the courtroom or through encounters with others. Further, sequestration can prevent leaks by jury members to reporters and others interested in the behind-the-scenes details of the trial.

Examination of Witnesses

Examination of witnesses is the questioning of witnesses during a trial by the prosecuting and defense attorneys for the purpose of establishing facts. When this is done initially, it is called direct examination. Cross-examination occurs when the opposing attorney asks questions intended to challenge the testimony elicited during direct examination. The attorney who performed the initial examination may then question the witness a second time in redirect examination, after which the opposing attorney has an opportunity for recross-examination. The judge may, to some extent, choose to control the type of questions asked -- for instance, if the questioning is redundant or vague.

Charging the Jury

Charging the jury is the step in the trial when the judge instructs the jury to retire to their chambers to decide on the guilt of the defendant. The judge uses this opportunity to explain the juror's duties and how they are expected to arrive at an opinion. It may include explanation of the laws that bear on the case and, in many instances, will include a recitation of the arguments made by the defense and the prosecution, as well as a recapitulation of the evidence that has been presented in the courtroom. Both the defense and prosecution lawyers are consulted by the judge in order to determine what should be presented. Ideally, the judge should inject no opinions of his or her own into the charge. In some cases, the charge to the jury can take several hours.

Pretrial Motions

Pretrial motions, as the term implies, occur before the beginning of the trial proper and sometimes before the arraignment. These are requests made of the court by both the defense and prosecution, and are designed to gain some advantage during the trial, by suppressing damaging evidence or changing the location of the trial. The most common pretrial motions are:

- Motion for discovery
- Motion for change of venue
- Motion for suppression
- Motion for a bill of particulars
- Motion for severance of charges or defendants
- Motion for continuance
- Motion for dismissal

Motion for Discovery

A motion for discovery is a pretrial motion filed by the defense that requests access to the evidence and names of witnesses that the prosecution plans to introduce during the trial. It is based in constitutional due process, but there has been some debate as to exactly how much discovery the Constitution requires. The Supreme Court ruled in 1963 that prosecutors could not refuse to disclose evidence in a trial, but in a later case the court decided that there is "no constitutional requirement that the prosecution make a complete and detailed accounting to the defense of all police investigatory work on a case" and that the failure to do so was not sufficient grounds in itself for an appeal.

MOTION FOR CHANGE OF VENUE

Sometimes either the prosecution or defense may decide that the venue -- that is, geographic area -- in which a trial is being held will not provide an unbiased jury and can request that the trial be moved to a different court at a different physical location. In this case, a pretrial motion for change of venue may be filed. The venue may also be changed if the initial venue is inconvenient in some way for the parties involved. The governing jurisdiction remains the same if this motion is granted, even though the location changes, even though it may be in a different city, county, or even state.

MOTION FOR SUPPRESSION

A motion for suppression is a pretrial motion that attempts to have certain pieces of evidence excluded from being presented during the trial. Such a motion is generally filed if there is reason to believe that the evidence may have been obtained in violation of due process -- e.g., through illegal search and seizure. The validity of a confession may be questioned and suppressed if it was deemed involuntary -- that is, obtained through some form of coercion and in violation of the suspect's constitutional rights. Alternatively, the method by which the evidence or confession was obtained may be presented to the jury during the trial so that they may decide if it is legitimate. Along with motion for dismissal, motion for suppression is one of the two most common pretrial motions.

MOTION FOR A BILL OF PARTICULARS

In criminal trials, a bill of particulars is a list of the claims that the prosecution will be making against the defendant. A pretrial motion for a bill of particulars allows the defense to determine what charges the defendant will be accused with so that they may prepare an adequate rebuttal to those charges in advance of the trial. The prosecution in a criminal trial may not file this motion (though it may be filed by the prosecution in a civil trial). This motion is not a request for disclosure of the evidence accompanying the charges.

MOTION FOR SEVERANCE OF CHARGES OR DEFENDANTS

A motion for severance of charges or defendants is a pretrial motion filed in cases where a defendant is being prosecuted under multiple charges or multiple counts of the same charge, or where multiple co-defendants are being charged with the same crime in the same trial. Often, the defense attorneys may feel that the defendant or defendants would be better served if each charge or co-defendant is prosecuted in a separate charge. This allows the defense to use separate tactics for each charge or defendant in front of separate juries. Studies have shown that juries are more likely to convict when multiple co-defendants are prosecuted in the same trial, so this motion is often seen as being to the benefit of the defendants.

MOTION FOR CONTINUANCE

A motion for continuance is a pretrial motion requesting that the trial be postponed in order to give either the prosecution or defense more time to prepare their case. This may be necessary if there has been insufficient time to find witnesses or acquire evidence. In some cases, the defense may use this motion as a way of repeatedly postponing the trial in the hope that witnesses, including the victim, may start to forget significant details or to force the prosecution to offer an advantageous plea bargain, although legitimate reasons for postponement would still be required and advantage alone is not sufficient for such a motion to be granted.

MOTION FOR DISMISSAL

A motion for dismissal is a pretrial motion that attempts to show that the prosecution has insufficient evidence to justify bringing the case to trial. This motion on the part of the defense is commonly filed at the arraignment and is usually dismissed by the judge. If a motion for suppression is successful at eliminating evidence that is considered crucial for the prosecution, it is possible that the prosecution itself will file this motion as an admission that they no longer have a strong enough case. (In many jurisdictions, this is the only way that the prosecution can drop charges against the defendant.) Along with motion for suppression, motion for dismissal is one of the two most common pretrial motions.

Selection of Eligible Jurors

Compiling a list of eligible jurors is the first step in the jury selection process. To be eligible a juror should be a US citizen, should not be a felon, should be an adult, and should not belong to professions excluded by law. (In some jurisdictions this includes attorneys, doctors, and others whose expertise may bias their opinions on the case.) Individual jurors may further ask for exemption for reasons of hardship based on employment or the need to take care of family members. In practice, the process begins with the local voter registration list is winnowed down based on these exceptions. The list compiled by this method is called the venire, a term that can also refer to the writ sent to jurors to summon them to jury duty.

Voir Dire

The voir dire is an oath sworn by jurors. It includes the opportunity for both defense and prosecution attorneys, as well as the judge, to examine (question) the potential jurors to see if something in their backgrounds might prejudice them either for or against the defendant. For instance, a juror may be acquainted with the defendant or have prejudicial familiarity with the case. Attorneys on both sides may exclude any jurors that they don't want to have on the panel. If the juror is challenged for cause, the challenging attorney must explain to the judge what their reasons are. If they make a peremptory challenge, no explanation is necessary. Studies have suggested that the voir dire is not an effective means of removing biased jurors from the panel.

Objection

An objection is made by either the defending or prosecuting attorneys when they feel that a question or line of questioning does not fit proper courtroom procedure. There are a large number of reasons for which an objection can be made. For instance, an attorney may object if they feel that a question is abusive to a witness or if they feel it leads a witness to respond with a particular answer. A question may be deemed argumentative if it attempts to have the witness draw conclusions based on facts rather than simply stating the facts. Objections are made to the judge, who may either sustain (support) them or overrule (dismiss) them.

Motion for a Directed Verdict

A motion for a directed verdict is filed by the defense after the prosecution has presented its case. It attempts to have the judge direct the jury to find the defendant not guilty on the grounds that the prosecution has failed to establish the defendant's guilt. The judge may also decide to do this without a motion, because evidence is inadequate, witnesses were not credible, or the prosecution conducted itself improperly. However, while the judge can direct the jury to find the defendant not guilty, he or she may not direct the jury to find the defendant guilty.

Closing Arguments

The closing arguments in a trial provide an opportunity for the defense and prosecution to summarize their arguments directly to the jury and refresh jurors' memory of the evidence and testimony presented during the trial. It is an opportunity for the attorneys to speak persuasively to the jury and attempt to sway them in ways that would not be considered appropriate during normal testimony. The defense may use this opportunity to poke holes in the prosecution's case.

Generally, the defense makes its argument first and the prosecution last. The eloquence of these attorneys and their skills at persuasive speaking are most important during this phase of the trial.

Jury Deliberations

After the defense and prosecution have made their closing statements, the jury retires to the jury room. The foreperson, who is either elected by the jurors or is simply the first juror selected, calls for a vote on the guilt of the defendant. If the vote is unanimous, the process is over. If not, the jury discusses the evidence and reviews the testimony before another vote is taken. If no consensus can be reached on the defendant's guilt, the jury is said to be deadlocked and a mistrial is declared, though this is unusual. Most juries take the time necessary to form an opinion and reach a unanimous verdict, though in some cases, jurors may be rushed by their schedules or a perceived need to be home for some special occasion such as a holiday.

Jury Nullification

Jury nullification is a decision on the part of the jury to find the defendant not guilty despite his or her clear violation of the law as it is interpreted by the court. It can occur because the jury finds the law unfair, because they think the penalties are too severe, or because they feel the defendant's actions were in some ways justified. The jurors may or may not intentionally be nullifying courtroom findings. If the jury finds the defendant guilty and the judge does not believe the decision is justified, the judge may nullify the verdict and charge the jury with acquitting the accused, but the judge may not nullify a verdict of not guilty no matter how ill-founded it may seem.

Post-Trial Motions

If the defendant is found guilty, the defense is given an opportunity to file post-trial motions. These are usually one of the following:

- a motion in arrest of judgment -- a request that the judgment be set aside because of an error in the case that is apparent in the record, including that the verdict was reached on charges that were not formally presented in the indictment;
- a motion for a new trial -- a request that a new trial be granted on grounds that the jury is tainted by outside information, that there was juror misconduct during deliberations, that the jury was tampered with (influenced by bribe or threat), that the judge improperly overruled an objection, or that there is new evidence available.

If the motion is granted, the trial is invalid, and a new trial can be held without constituting double jeopardy.

Subpoena

A subpoena is a written order produced by a court commanding testimony from a witness. Subpoenas are produced by court clerks or by lawyers acting in the capacity of court clerks. This is done in the name of a judge or a grand jury. There are two types of testimony: subpoena ad testificandu, in which testimony is commanded, and subpoena duces tecum, in which the recipient is commanded to produce an item or items of physical evidence. Subpoenas carry the full force of law, and failure to comply with a subpoena can result in legal punishment.

Release on Recognizance

Release on recognizance (or ROR) refers to the release from detention of a criminal suspect pending trial on the promise of returning for the trial and for any other stages of the criminal justice process where the individual is scheduled to appear. It may be conditioned on remaining within a certain geographic region, remaining in the presence of some responsible party, or periodically reporting to the court. No bail or bond is required. Release on recognizance is generally granted because the suspect is not deemed dangerous and has strong personal ties to the community that preclude an attempt to evade prosecution. The seriousness of the crime itself is also a consideration.

RAPE SHIELD LAWS

Rape shield laws are rules that have been passed in the majority of jurisdictions concerning the questions that can be asked during the cross-examination of the victim during a rape trial. Specifically, these rules ban questions concerning the victim's previous sexual experiences. These laws were mostly passed in the 1970s, out of concern that the rape victims themselves were being tried and accused during trials that should instead focus on the actions of the rapist. It was especially feared that the judgment of jurors would become affected if they perceived the woman as promiscuous, a factor not relevant to the fact of rape. Data on the effectiveness of rape shield laws are not conclusive, however, and there is some fear that they may violate rights of due process.

INDETERMINATE SENTENCE

An indeterminate sentence is a sentence that will take place not over a single, fixed period but over a possible range of time, defined by a maximum and a minimum sentence. Indeterminate sentences allow the actual amount of time served to be tailored to the particular offender and that offender's behavior after imprisonment. After the minimum time has been served, a parole board assesses evidence that the prisoner has made progress toward rehabilitation. The law itself contains guidelines for what the range of time should be for different crimes, with the judge given leeway to set a specific range within those limitations based on the particulars of the case.

DETERMINATE SENTENCE AND DEFINITE SENTENCE

Under a determinate sentence, the length of sentence for a specific type of crime is established by law, and the judge has no discretion to change that length (though the judge may still choose various forms of sentence, including probation and fine). A parole board can still shorten the duration of some types of determinate sentence, according to law. A definite sentence is a type of determinate sentence in which the length is fixed by law and cannot be shortened by a parole board. This type of sentence, common in the 1920s, became uncommon for many years, but was revived in the 1970s as definite, or "flat," sentences became popular in many states.

MANDATORY SENTENCE

A mandatory sentence is a sentence prescribed by law for a specific crime that may not be altered by a judge if a defendant is convicted of such a crime. Mandatory sentences have been common in recent years for violation of drug laws, but it has been found that these sentences are often unnecessary because in serious cases these sentences would be used by most judges anyway, and in other cases they can lead to unnecessarily severe punishment for less serious offenders. In some cases, the sentences are also arbitrary and frequently exist for political reasons more than for judicial ones.

PLEA NEGOTIATION

A plea negotiation (or, as it is more popularly known, a plea bargain) is a process by which a prosecutor and a defendant (or that defendant's attorney) can work out the defendant's plea (usually a guilty plea) in advance of a trial. It involves securing a guilty plea in return for certain concessions by the government for the defendant, either a reduction of the charges, a reduction of the number of counts for each charge, a recommendation of leniency to the court, or a change in terminology to a less offensive sounding (but equally serious crime), e.g., child molestation being changed to assault. Plea negotiation helps to reduce the load on overcrowded courts, reduces the cost of prosecution, and takes care of less serious cases that should not be demanding the court's attention.

Probation

Probation is a form of sentence imposed on a convicted criminal who is not considered dangerous and for whom prison would be both unnecessary and a possible gateway to a criminal career. When sentenced to probation, the offender has certain rights temporarily taken away and is expected to abide by certain rules, but is given an opportunity to demonstrate that, if allowed to live outside prison, he or she will become a law-abiding citizen and can be trusted not to engage in irresponsible or criminal behavior. Probation often begins with a suspended sentence, that is, a sentence that is not carried out as long as the offender behaves. Certain conditions of probation are generally imposed, and the offender is expected to report regularly to a probation officer.

Suspended sentence

A suspended sentence is a power granted to judges to suspend the imposition of a sentence on a convicted offender and instead allow the offender to demonstrate their willingness to live a law-abiding and responsible life during a probationary period. The suspended sentence may be revoked at the judgment of the court, generally on the basis of the offender's behavior during probation, at which point a full sentence will be passed. Generally, the suspended sentence will be revoked if the offender commits a new offence during the probationary period or violates the terms of probation. The suspended sentence is often used as a means of alleviating prison overcrowding, but can also be seen as a tool for rehabilitation and as a way of preventing a prison sentence from turning a first-time offender into a hardened criminal.

Restitution programs

Restitution programs allow convicted criminals to correct some of the damage caused by their crimes by paying some form of compensation to the victims or performing services for the community in which the crime was committed. It's a way in which convicted offenders can take responsibility for their crime and serve in providing justice. Restitution programs also represent a reasonable alternative to paying a fine, which would go to the state rather than the victim. They are controversial because they can give convicted offenders a sense that what they did was "okay" as long as they make payments, and because they unfairly favor relatively well-to-do offenders who can afford to make the payments. Community service as a form of restitution, because it is available to everyone no matter their income, helps to correct the latter imbalance.

Shock probation

Shock probation is a relatively new form of sentencing based on the concept that the first few days in prison have almost as much deterrent effect for first-time detainees as a full prison sentence. Shock probation involves a prison stay of a month or two followed by probation. The premise is that once a convicted offender has seen the inside of a prison they will be less likely to violate their probation because their fear of the subsequent imprisonment will be enhanced. It is controversial, in part because one of the purposes of probation is to prevent the offender from becoming part of prison life and forming associations that will lead to a criminal career. Further, the National Institute for Justice has concluded that it is ineffective at preventing future criminal behavior.

Corrections

Punishment in Colonial America

These are all forms of punishment imposed in Colonial America. They are defined as follows:

- Bilboe -- An iron bar with metal loops that could be placed over the offender's legs and then tightened to inflict pain.
- Brank -- A cage-like device fitted over the offender's head such that a plate could be placed in the mouth that caused pain with speaking.
- Dunking stool -- A chair placed on a large lever next to a river. The person being punished would be lowered repeatedly into the water.
- Scarlet letter -- Bright red letters worn by offenders according to their offense, with an "A" worn by adulterers, "B" by blasphemers, "D" by drunkards, "P" by paupers, "T" by thieves, and so forth.
- Stocks and pillory -- Wooden frames into which a person's head, hands, and feet could be inserted and locked in place.

Corporal punishment

Corporal punishment is punishment in which pain is inflicted, but not death. These punishments include flogging, having body parts such as hands removed, castration, and various forms of torture. They are often designed to be appropriate to the crime that was committed, so that castration would be used to punish rapists, having a hand cut off would be punishment for theft, blasphemy would be punished by cutting off the blasphemer's tongue, and so forth. Corporal punishments imposed by court were once common and still occur in some parts of the world, but are not used in the United States.

Walnut Street Jail

The Walnut Street Jail was built in Pennsylvania in 1776, and in its time was at the forefront of prison reform. It was the first penitentiary in the United States, built by a Quaker organization called the Philadelphia Society for Alleviating the Miseries of Public Prisons as a place where criminals could "repent" from their crimes. Cells were given high ceilings, and windows were placed where prisoners could not look out. Prisoners were not put to work as in other prisons, but given long periods in solitary confinement so that they could reflect on their actions. The Walnut Street Jail introduced the so-called Pennsylvania Model of prison design.

Separate system

The separate system was a 19th century system of prison management that emphasized solitary confinement. It was based on the idea that allowing prisoners to associate with one another in prison bred more crime and produced hardened criminals. Criminals left alone, it was thought, would have time to contemplate their crimes and reflect on the nature of their wrongdoings. Further, it simplified disciplinary actions and made it possible to tailor punishments specifically to the individual prisoners. Because criminals did not associate while imprisoned, they were unlikely to form criminal alliances once released. The first prison based on this philosophy, built in 1829, was the Eastern State Penitentiary in Philadelphia.

Silent system

The silent system was a 19th century prison philosophy in which prisoners were allowed to work together, but not allowed to speak. All prison labor took place in silence. This enforced silence supposedly prevented criminals from influencing one another or plotting escape. Unlike the separate system, it emphasized hard labor, which was believed essential not only to criminal reform but the economic survival of the prison. Corporal punishment was used to enforce discipline. This system was first used at Auburn Prison in New York State in 1823. Prisoners at Auburn were given striped uniforms both to humiliate them and to make them more identifiable. An isolation wing known as "the hole" was available for prisoners being punished for violating prison rules.

Reformatory Philosophy of Alexander Maconochie

Alexander Maconochie was the director of the Norfolk Island penal colony from 1840 to 1844. He was a key figure in the 19th century Reformatory Era of prisons. His philosophy of prison reform consisted of five principles:

1. Prison sentences should not be for a length of time, but for a quantity of work to be performed by the prisoner.
2. Prisoners should work for "marks" by adopting good conduct and positive living principles during their incarceration. This is called the mark system.
3. Prisoners should use their marks, or go into a debt for a number of marks, to purchase everything they need in prison, including food.
4. Prisoners should work in groups where each member is accountable for the group's conduct.
5. After a certain amount of time, prisoners should be given a share of their earnings and be prepared for return to normal society.

Sir Walter Crofton's "Irish System"

Sir Walter Crofton was a prison administrator in mid-19th century Ireland and a leader in the Reformatory Movement. He introduced what came to be called the Irish System, which involved putting convicts through a progressive sequence of steps:

1. Two years of solitary confinement and work;
2. A mark system similar to that used by Alexander Maconochie at the Norfolk Island penal colony, where prisoners could use their work to acquire privileges and shorten their prison stay;
3. A work-leave program where prisoners worked outside the prison once they had served their period of working within the prison;
4. A ticket-of-leave, which allows the prisoner to be released through a system similar to modern parole.

Reformatory at Elmira, New York

The reformatory at Elmira, New York, which opened in 1876, incorporated the reformatory philosophies of Alexander Maconochie and Sir Walter Crofton. Under Superintendent Zebulon Brockman, it incorporated a set of principles that came to be known as The Elmira System. These included sanitary facilities for the prisoners, non-degrading uniforms, a good diet, modern exercise and athletic equipment, training in several skills, classes up through high school and even college, a library, a prison newspaper produced by prisoners, entertainment, religious services, and "emotional occasions" (planned, non-instructional events). Although some of Brockway's principles were never put into practice at the prison, the model created by the Elmira Reformatory proved influential and spread to other prisons.

Reformatory Era

The Reformatory Era began in the 1940s with Alexander Maconochie's work at the Norfolk Island penal colony and was later developed by Irish penal director Sir Walter Crofton and Zebulon Brockman at the Elmira Reformatory in Elmira, New York. It emphasized the education and reformation of prisoners so that they could return to private life as honest citizens. To this end, the prison experience was made less degrading, facilities were made more sanitary, and prisoners were given the ability to work for privileges and shortened sentences (the "mark system"). The Reformatory Era was in many ways a failure (Prisoners were used to a different system of punishment, prisons were overcrowded, and there were shortages of prison staff.), and attempts at using the systems developed by these men were abandoned by 1910. Nonetheless, the reform movement was influential on later developments in prisons.

Industrial Prisons of the Early 20th Century

By the beginning of the 20th century, most American prisons were founded on an industrial model. Inmate labor was used for the production of saleable goods. This was both a means of correction and a way in which the prison system could be self sustaining. There was, however, a backlash to this system by organized labor, which felt that it was unfair to private businesses and non-prison labor. In addition, many prison reformers felt that this system was exploitative. A series of laws were passed from the late 1920 to the early 1940s limiting the ability of prisons to profit from the sale of prisoner-made goods.

The Hawes-Cooper Act, the Ashurst-Sumners Act, and the Walsh-Healy Act

These were a series of acts by Congress that restricted the ability of prisons to sell goods manufactured by prisoners.

- The Hawes-Cooper Act of 1929 -- Taking effect in 1934, this act allowed states to ban the import of prison-made goods from other states. (States already had the right to ban the sale of goods made at prisons in their own state.)
- The Ashurst-Sumners Act of 1935 -- This act made it a federal offense to transport prison-made goods into states that had banned their import.
- The Walsh-Healy Act of 1936 -- This act banned almost all interstate transport of prison-made goods.

Attica Prison Revolt

In 1971, conditions at the Attica Correctional Facility in Attica, New York, were harsh. Rules and regulations were strict, prisoners were locked in their cells for much of the day, food was poor, showers were available once a week, both family visitations and visits to the bathroom were closely monitored, and little vocational training was available. Available clothing was poor, and the budget for supplies was limited. Racial tensions were rife, because the prison population was mostly African-American or Hispanic and the prison staff was almost entirely white. Early in September 1971, inmates openly revolted, spreading through the prison and taking hostages. Eventually police forced the prisoners into the exercise yard, but they continued to hold 39 people hostage. On September 13th, police troopers retook the prison, killing 29 prisoners and 10 hostages in the process. The Attica revolt served to put a spotlight on the issue of prisoners' rights.

Arkansas Prison Scandal

In 1968, it was revealed that conditions in Arkansas prisons were stark and inhumane. Prisoners were routinely beaten, tortured, and even murdered for disciplinary infractions. Arkansas prison officials bragged that their system was self-supporting, but this turned out to be the result of an exploitative prison labor system and the use of inmate "trusties" who were given special (and often illegal) privileges as they effectively ran the system with little help from traditional guards. These conditions came to light when criminologist Thomas O. Murton, a professor at Southern Illinois University, was put in charge of the prison system by Arkansas governor Winthrop Rockefeller. In the case Holt v. Sarver, a federal court ruled that these conditions violated the Eighth Amendment prohibition of cruel and unusual punishment.

New Mexico Inmate Massacre

In the late 1970s, it was found by an investigatory committee that conditions in the New Mexico State Penitentiary were unsanitary, that the prison was understaffed, and that medical care was inadequate. In February 1980, almost a thousand inmates at the New Mexico State Penitentiary rioted and seized control of the facility, taking 15 hostages. They demanded improvements in prison conditions and that prison officials stop harassing the prisoners over their complaints. They threatened to kill the hostages if these demands were not met. When negotiations failed, an assault by police and the New Mexico National Guard ended the riot, but not until after at least 33 prisoners had been killed by the prisoners themselves as an act of revenge. The killings were unusually brutal and included a beheading. Other prisoners died in the assault that retook the prison.

Ruiz v. Estelle

In the 1972 Federal court case Ruiz v. Estelle, an inmate of the Texas Department of Corrections named David Ruiz sued the prison director over the conditions in the prison system, citing overcrowding, inadequate security, unsafe working conditions, inadequate healthcare, and severe disciplinary measures. The court ruled that prison conditions were "pernicious," that inmates in the system had "justifiable fears", and that reforms on the part of the prison system were necessary. Despite this decision being upheld by a higher court, it took a decade for significant reforms to appear in the Texas prison system, which officials argued was the best in the country.

Rehabilitation in the Criminal Justice System

Rehabilitation is the return of criminals to general society with the criminal elements of their behavior modified or removed. It is based on the idea that criminals can lead productive, honest lives when returned to general society if the roots of their behavior are addressed and altered so that the behavior, and the need for that behavior, is eliminated. There is some debate as to what role rehabilitation should play in the sentencing of criminals, with some arguing that it is the most effective use of the criminal justice system, others arguing that the roots of crime are not understood well enough for true rehabilitation to be effected, and still others believing that rehabilitation is simply neither possible nor necessary, and that the criminal justice system should emphasize deterrence and proportional retribution instead.

Within the prison system, a number of activities are available for inmates to help them reenter normal society. These include:

- Treatment programs -- These are psychological treatment programs that attempt to socialize the prisoner and modify their behavior away from antisocial activities.
- Academic and vocational programs -- These are educational programs that impart skills which will prove useful in securing employment and earning a living through noncriminal activities.
- Recreational programs -- These are programs involving recreational activities that will socialize prisoners and decrease hostility.
- Work programs -- These are employment programs within the prison that both serve to rehabilitate the prisoner through gainful work and to finance prison activities.

Most prisons also have medical and religious programs available for prisoners.

Retribution in Criminal Justice

Retribution is the idea there should be a proportional relationship between a crime and its punishment -- or, in the words of 18th century philosopher Cesare, Marquis of Beccaria, society should try "to make the punishment as analogous as possible to nature of the crime." This differs from the philosophy of "an eye for an eye and a tooth for a tooth" in that it is not necessary to inflict the same act upon the criminal that the criminal has exacted upon the victim but that the punishment is proportional, with the most serious crimes having the most severe punishments.

Deterrence in the Criminal Justice System

Deterrence is one of the most important functions of the criminal justice system. It prevents crimes in the future by demonstrating in the present that criminal acts will be met with justice and punishment. There are two kinds of deterrence:

- General deterrence is the function of the criminal justice system to deter all crime by demonstrating to society at large that punishment will be swift and effective.
- Specific deterrence is aimed at convincing the individual offenders that future crimes on their part will be punished.

Studies have shown convincingly that punishment does deter crime, but that some types of crime are more easily deterred than others. In addition, the inevitability of punishment is more important to deterrence than the actual severity of the punishment.

Parole

Parole is the release from prison of a convicted offender who has served the minimum sentence imposed by the court, but not the maximum sentence, on the judgment of authorities that he or she has been sufficiently rehabilitated to reenter life outside prison. Parole allows authorities to tailor sentences to the individual. It also reduces prison overcrowding and provides prison officials with a means of punishment for violation of regulations, in that they can threaten revocation of parole for bad behavior. Parole is bestowed by a parole board at a parole hearing. Although ostensibly parole is granted when it is felt that the interests of the community have been served by the prisoner's sentence, it is sometimes granted or denied capriciously or for political reasons.

Parole Board

Parole boards decide when to grant parole to a prisoner who has served his or her minimum sentence, supervise the activities of the prisoner after release into the community, determine when parole has been fully served, and decide if a violation has occurred that justifies revoking parole. Parole members are chosen for a number of reasons, but are generally expected to be respected members of their community and to have knowledge of the law, behavioral science, and corrections. According to the National Advisory Commission on Criminal Justice and Goals, parole board members should be "persons with sophisticated training and experience." Nonetheless, parole board members are sometimes inexperienced in relevant areas.

Parole Hearings

Parole hearings are where it is decided whether a prisoner is to be granted parole. The prisoner attends, as does the parole board. An official of the prison is usually also in attendance. A stenographer records the proceedings. Data available for the parole board to make its decision include records of the prisoner's court proceedings and any records of their behavior during incarceration. According to court rulings, due process does not apply at a parole hearing, and the exclusionary rule is not applicable to the evidence presented. However, if parole is denied the prisoner must receive a written list of the reasons for denial.

INTENSIVE PROBATION SUPERVISION

Intensive probation supervision is a form of probation in which the probationer is supervised much more closely than in regular probation. This may include several meetings per week between the probationer and the probation officer, community service, employment required by the court, curfews, and drug testing. Intensive probation supervision is an alternative to imprisonment for convicted offenders who would not ordinarily be considered as eligible for parole. Intensive probation supervision is an old concept that has generated renewed interest in recent years. Opinions are mixed as to its effectiveness. However, it has the advantage of being more cost-effective than incarceration.

PAROLE PREDICTION

Parole prediction attempts to use statistical methods to foresee the probability that an inmate will violate parole. It uses tables of data that group offenders according by characteristics and likelihood of committing crime when released from prison. These methods and tables have been in use since the 1930s, but are controversial. Proponents argue that they are a valuable tool for use by parole boards, while opponents make the counter-argument that they are not a good way to predict individual behavior because the variables that are taken into account by the tables are not necessarily the most predictive and the tables rely too heavily on presentencing reports without sufficiently taking into account the offender's behavior in prison. There is no evidence that parole prediction is any more accurate at predicting recidivism than parole systems that rely on case studies and the judgment of the parole board.

MANDATORY RELEASE AND GOOD TIME

Good time is earned by prison inmates for time served without problems and for participation in programs and for service beyond the call of duty. When a certain number of good time days have been accumulated by a prisoner, they are given mandatory release. Mandatory release is similar to parole, but it is not left to the decision of a parole board and, in most states, is an unconditional release not subject to the same supervision and conditions as parole. Mandatory release helps solve the problem of parole being denied for political reasons or because of the bias of either the parole board or those consulted by the parole board.

PAROLE CONDITIONS

Parole is a conditional release from prison. Certain conditions must be met by the parolee or the parole will be revoked and the parolee will be returned to prison. Some of these conditions involve the individual's behavior while on parole. For instance, they generally must refrain from breaking the law and from using illegal drugs. Parole is often made contingent on having a job. There are also conditions that require reporting regularly to a parole officer and asking the parole officer's permission before moving or quitting a job. Specific conditions vary between jurisdictions. Some of these conditions, such as those that abridge First Amendment rights, have over time been found by the court to be unconstitutional.

DISCHARGE FROM PAROLE

Parole discharge occurs when the parolee no longer has to follow the terms of parole and can no longer have parole revoked and be returned to prison. It can occur for a number of reasons. For instance, parole discharge occurs when the maximum sentencing period has elapsed. Alternatively, many jurisdictions set a minimum parole period, after which parole can be discharged if the parolee's behavior is deemed satisfactory by the parole board. It is also possible during parole that the parolee can be pardoned for the crime for which they are serving the sentence or have the sentence commuted, in which case parole discharge is immediate. Once parole has been discharged, the offender regains the full civil rights of a free citizen (though in some jurisdictions convicted prisoners still retain their full civil rights while the sentence is being served).

Revocation of Parole

A paroled offender may at any time have their parole revoked and be returned to prison or to supervision. The amount of the sentence that remains for the offender to serve can then be decided in a number of different ways. Many parole boards give credit for street time, which is usually the amount of time served after the parolee is released from prison until parole is violated. The parole board can then set a length of time before parole can again be considered for the offender. In some jurisdictions, the offender is required to serve the rest of his/her sentence without having street time deducted from it, on the premise that the sentence was not being served while on parole.

Home Furlough

A home furlough is a temporary release from prison that can be granted to an inmate for a number of purposes, including education, job interviews, maintaining family relationships and solving family problems, or preparing for release from prison. It is part of the rehabilitative process and allows the prisoner to keep their life in order so he/she can reenter society with minimal difficulty once released. Home furlough is only used in some jurisdictions and is subject to varying requirements and conditions according to local statute. It is frequently restricted to only those prisoners with a good record or those who are nearing the time at which they can be considered for parole.

Work Release

Work release is a form of prisoner furlough in which an inmate is allowed to leave the prison to work at a paying job within the community, but must continue to live and serve time within the prison. It is an old idea, going back to 1913, that has gained increased popularity over the last 40 years and is now commonly used in a large number of jurisdictions. Work release is typically restricted to offenders who have shown good behavior and who will soon be eligible for parole. Work release helps prepare the prisoner for release, both by improving the prisoner's self-image and by giving the prisoner a means of support once released. It also allows prisoners to support their families and to become part of the local economy. Work release is not always effective. Prisons are frequently located at a distance from the job market, and employers are not always interested in having convicted convicts as employees.

Religious Programs for Inmates

The encouragement of religion of prisoners has long been seen as a means of rehabilitation, but it is a controversial one. Most prisons have some type of chaplain who can perform religious services and provide religious training for interested inmates. Whether this actually has much in the way of rehabilitative effect has never been determined. Inmates are often skeptical of the religious opportunities being afforded them and see these services as insincere at best. Service as a chaplain is not highly valued by most clerics, though some religious institutions have taken on the prisoner outreach as their mission. Many prison officials believe strongly that religion is a valid correctional tool, and some prisoners have embraced religion as a means of avoiding despair while incarcerated.

Prison Medical Services and Facilities

Medical facilities are an important part of the prison system, though they vary from barely adequate to large-scale hospital units that include surgical facilities. Most prisons have at least a small medical staff available. Because of their confined spaces and large populations, prisons are a perfect milieu for the spread of disease, including AIDS, and controlling that spread is important. Proper medical care is also an important element of inmate rehabilitation and, in many cases, may include drug treatment for chronic drug abusers. The institutional medical staff also oversees prisoner nutrition and sanitation.

Educational Programs for Prison Inmates

Because prison inmates tend to have a relatively low educational level, education programs for inmates are required by most states. These programs generally emphasize basic education in two categories: academic and vocational. In academic programs, prisoners are taught basic literacy and given an opportunity to earn high school equivalency degrees. At some prisons, college-level courses are available. In vocational programs, prisoners are taught skills that will allow them to gain employment after release in areas such as automobile mechanics, electrical work, plumbing, carpentry, and electronics. These programs are often limited by inadequate facilities in the prison, and the quality of the teachers may not be as high as in non-prison educational systems. Nonetheless, there is evidence that inmates who participate in these programs are less likely to commit crimes after leaving prison than those inmates who do not seek education while incarcerated.

Drug Abuse Treatment in Prison

As much as 75 percent of prisoners in the United States have a history of drug abuse. In many cases these prisoners are incarcerated for drug-related crimes. For this reason, some prisons have a separate housing facility for drug treatment known as a therapeutic community or TC. Inmates in a TC have their own facilities, medical treatment, schools, recreation, and work separate from other prisoners. Group therapy sessions are held regularly. Therapeutic communities are found outside of the prison environment as well. They are the product of work done in the 1940s by British psychiatrist Maxwell Jones.

Solitary Confinement

Solitary confinement is a punishment frequently inflicted on prison inmates for violations of prison rules and regulations. It involves being placed in a small cell in isolation from the rest of the prison population and may also entail beatings, loss of rights and privileges, and a restricted diet. Despite claims that solitary confinement represents cruel and unusual punishment, the courts have generally been reluctant to ban it because it represents a form of discipline generally deemed necessary within the prison system. However, the courts have placed certain restrictions on the duration of the confinement, as well as the hygienic and dietary conditions involved.

Lockdown

A lockdown is a situation in a prison where prisoners are confined to cells and not allowed to participate in normal activities outside the cell, including seeing visitors, exercising, eating meals in a cafeteria area, or socializing with other prisoners. It is usually performed in an emergency situation, such as a prison riot or other disruptive event, when officials need to maintain or regain control of the facility. For instance, lockdowns can occur if a fight breaks out between inmates or a guard is assaulted. The term can also be used colloquially to describe the prison facility itself, especially a high-security facility.

Open Institutions

Open institutions are facilities in which young offenders can work at a profession such as farming or forestry. They often include vocational training that attempts to move offenders toward gainful employment. Prison uniforms are usually not required in an open institution. The prisoners are generally paid for their efforts and are given leisure time, often with recreational facilities available.

These facilities come in specific types geared toward specific kinds of work or training. For instance, they may be forestry camps or ranches. Open institutions are economical, relieve population pressure on conventional prisons, and can produce products used throughout the prison system. Many state parks are maintained at least in part by the inmates of these facilities.

Significance of Schall v. Martin

In the 1984 Supreme Court case Schall v. Martin, the high court dealt with the issue of juvenile detention. The case involved the practice of preventive detention, in which an accused juvenile offender is held in custody by the government while his/her case is being processed because it is feared that he/she will commit further crimes before the case is decided. The case resulted from a writ of habeas corpus filed by a 14-year-old detainee named Gregory Martin on behalf of all juvenile offenders. The court ruled that detention of a juvenile is not unreasonable under certain circumstances because "juveniles, unlike adults, are always in some form of custody.... Children, by definition, are not assumed to have the capacity to take care of themselves."

Roper v. Simmons

In the 2005 Supreme Court case Roper v. Simmons, a convict on death row appealed his sentence to the court on the grounds that he had only been 17 at the time he committed murder, and that sentencing a juvenile to death constituted a violation of Eighth Amendment protections against cruel and unusual punishment. The court agreed and overturned the sentence. In its decision, Justice Anthony Kennedy wrote that "[w]hen a juvenile commits a heinous crime, the State can exact forfeiture of some of the most basic liberties, but the State cannot extinguish his life and his potential to attain a mature understanding of his own humanity."

Gregg v. Georgia

In the 1976 Supreme Court case Gregg v. Georgia, the high court returned to the issue of inconsistency in the application of the death penalty which had been previously discussed in the 1972 case Furman v. Georgia. Since Furman, states had been revising their death penalty statutes in light of court guidelines that such statutes must use objective criteria for imposing capital punishment and must take into account the record of the defendant. In Gregg, the court further ruled that a separate hearing was necessary in capital cases for deciding whether the death penalty should be imposed. At the time of this case no death sentences had been carried out in the United States for four years, a de facto moratorium that ended with Gregg.

Furman v. Georgia

In the 1972 Supreme Court case Furman v. Georgia, the high court dealt with the issue of consistency in the application of the death penalty and whether inconsistent application of the death penalty constituted cruel and unusual punishment. In this case, William Henry Furman had fatally shot a man in Georgia during in burglary, a capital offense under Georgia law. The case was appealed on the grounds that the death penalty is imposed arbitrarily, and the majority of the court agreed, though only two justices felt that the death penalty is actually unconstitutional. Over the next several years states began revising death penalty statutes to make application of the death penalty more consistent. As a result, no death sentences were carried out between the time of this case and 1976.

Coker v. Georgia

In the 1977 Supreme Court case Coker v. Georgia, the high court dealt with the issue of whether imposing the death penalty for rape represented a violation of Eighth Amendment protections against cruel and unusual punishment. The defendant, Coker, had been convicted of committing rape during the course of armed robbery and was sentenced to death. The court ruled that the sentence was disproportionate -- that is, the punishment was too severe for the crime -- and it is this lack of proportionality that makes it cruel and unusual punishment.

McCleskey v. Kemp

The 1987 Supreme Court case McCleskey v. Kemp, the high court dealt with racial disparities in the application of the death penalty. The case concerned an African American man, Warren McCloskey, who had been sentenced to death for killing a police officer. McCleskey appealed the case on the grounds that a study had suggested that the death penalty was more likely to be imposed in cases where the accused is black, particularly when the victim is white. The court found the statistics on these disparities unconvincing and upheld McCleskey's sentence.

Atkins v. Virginia

In the 2002 Supreme Court case Atkins v. Virginia, the court dealt with the issue of capital punishment for the intellectually disabled. The defendant, Atkins, had robbed a man and then killed him. Although Atkins was judged intellectually disabled, he was sentenced to death on the basis of previous convictions and the viciousness of the crime. The Supreme Court reviewed the case because of changing attitudes concerning the execution of the mentally incompetent. The court ruled that because most state legislatures had rejected such executions, there was a national consensus that executing the intellectually disabled was wrong, and that such executions represented a "needless imposition of pain and suffering." The sentence was overturned.

Ring v. Arizona

In the 2002 Supreme Court case Ring v. Arizona, the court considered the issue of who should impose the death penalty in a case: the judge or the jury. In Ring, the defendant had been convicted of murder under the felony-murder doctrine, which holds that any murder committed during the commission of a felony, even if intent is lacking, is a capital crime. Normally, the jury verdict of first-degree murder would have resulted, under Arizona law, in a life sentence at most. The court felt that the jury, rather than the judge, should have been allowed to determine the "sentencing factors" that would have increased the sentence. This decision overturned sentencing laws in four states and cast doubt on other laws, even where the judge's decision is based on a jury recommendation.

Jail and Prison

In the United States, a jail is a local detention facility used to hold both suspected criminals awaiting trial and convicted criminals who are serving short sentences, usually up to one year. Typically these sentences are for misdemeanor offenses. Jails are usually operated by a local, typically a city or county. There are more than 3500 jails across the US Prisons are larger facilities operated either by a state or the federal government. They are used to hold felons for longer sentences. Prisons run by the federal government's Bureau of Prisons operate at three different levels of security, with a fourth level of security at some prisons. This level is known as supermax. These maximum security prisons hold the most dangerous offenders. Supermax facilities may represent part or the entirety of a prison. A fifth level of security, known as an open institution, is a kind of work facility for prisoners who need minimal security.

Federal Prisons

Federal prisons can be grouped by level of security. The three traditional levels are minimum-security, medium-security and maximum-security.

- Minimum-security prisons -- These prisons are used to house criminals considered nonviolent and trustworthy. They have no security guards, no walls, and often no security fences. They often do not resemble conventional prisons, but can be arranged as dormitories or even as small villages with stores, churches, and schools.
- Medium-security prisons -- These are more conventional prison structures with walls, fences, and a general fortress-like appearance. Many cells are located on the outside (i.e., facing the prison yard) and may share living facilities. There are usually fewer guards than in a maximum-security prison.
- Maximum-security prisons -- These are prisons that house violent and dangerous criminals. They are surrounded by multiple levels of fences, often electrified, with cells concentrated on the inside, with no access to the prison yard. They are heavily guarded.

Supermax Prisons

Supermax prisons are a relatively recent variation on maximum security prisons. They are usually special units within a maximum security prison, though entire prisons can be designated as supermax. These facilities hold especially violent criminals, who are usually kept in isolation. These criminals include those who have a history of violence while imprisoned as well as those who have a history of either escaping or attempting to escape from prison. Supermax prisons include the federal Administrative Maximum Facility in Florence, Colorado. Supermax prisons may include stepdown facilities, where prisoners can learn to be more social in preparation for a return to the normal prison population.

Reception Center

When an inmate first enters the prison system, they are sent to an institution called a reception center where they can be evaluated and given an orientation to the system. This is where classification takes place, a process that can take up to a month. The staff is specifically trained in this process and makes recommendations about the needs of each prisoner that are passed on to officials at the specific institutions to which each prisoner is eventually sent. In some cases the reception center can also serve as a medical center for inmates.

Classification of Prisoners

The classification of prisoners allows the prison system to determine the specific needs of each prisoner. Classification includes determining the level of security needed for the prisoner from a minimum-security prison or even open institution to a maximum-security or supermax facility. Classification may also include decisions as to what kind of job the prisoner can perform while in prison. The medical condition of the prisoner may also be ascertained. In the federal system and in some state systems, the prisoner is initially placed in a reception center, where he/she remains for a few weeks to three months while classification is performed. In most prisons a classification committee is responsible for the classifying of prisoners. However, many characteristics of prisoner are not generally classified, such as their security and treatment needs, which can lead to inappropriate mixtures of inmates within the prison, such as vulnerable young prisoners placed with violent older ones.

Elderly Prisoners

The average age of prisoners in the American prison system has increased dramatically in recent years. This is in part due to the aging of the general population in a time where medical advances have greatly extended life expectancies, but it is also the result of changes in sentencing laws that have made it more likely that prisoners will spend their entire lives in the prison system. Elderly prisoners are expensive to maintain because they have medical needs that the rest of the prison population does not. Many prisons have taken the precaution of moving elderly prisoners into special sections of the prison, where they can be given special care and where they are not endangered by younger, violent offenders.

Mentally-ill Patients

The mentally ill represent a large portion of the prison population. This reflects a change that has taken place over the last 40 years in the way the mentally ill have been treated by society. Until the late 1960s, people with severe psychological disorders were likely to remain in mental institutions for most of their lives, but the development of powerful antipsychotic drugs resulted in the de-institutionalization of much of this population. Unfortunately, many of these people ultimately ended up in prison. The prison system is only partially equipped to deal with mentally-ill patients, who need special care and medication. Some mentally-ill people do well in prison, but many end their sentences with suicide or are tormented by other prisoners. Only a few prisons have developed special facilities for dealing with the mentally unstable.

Adaptations Made by Male Inmates

The most common adaptations to prison life made by male inmates are:

5. "Doing time" -- The inmate accepts the prison stay as inevitable and tries to get along by obeying prison rules, adapting to the inmate code of behavior, and surviving as best he can until release.
6. "Gleaning" -- The inmate uses prison time as an opportunity to improve himself through prison education programs and correspondence courses. This helps the prisoner to have a better, rehabilitated life after prison.
7. "Jailing" -- The inmate adapts so thoroughly to prison life that life outside the prison no longer seems important and attempts to excel within prison culture.
8. "Disorganized criminal" -- The inmate is unable to adapt to prison and becomes largely dysfunctional.

Prisoner Labor Systems

These are systems by which prisoner labor has been organized in prison industries. They work as follows:

- Contract system -- Prison labor is supervised by outside contractors who pay the prison system for the use of its inmates.
- Piece-price system -- Prison labor remains under the supervision of the prisons, but outside contractors pay for the product.
- Lease system -- Contractors take complete responsibility for prisoners, including their food and housing.
- State-account plan -- Prison labor remains under the control of the prison, which markets the product and gives a share of the profit to prisoners.
- State-use plan -- Prison labor remains under the control of the prison, but the products of the labor are used by the government itself.

Sexual Assault

The frequency of sexual assaults that occur in the prison community is the subject of some debate. Same-sex rape in prison is popularly thought to be quite common, particularly in men-only prisons, though the few studies on the subject have suggested that the frequency of such assaults is rather low. When such assault does occur, it is usually a means of establishing dominance or asserting manhood rather than for any kind of sexual pleasure. Sexual harassment by prison administrators, mostly by male administrators of female prisoners, seems to be somewhat common and often involves the exchange of sexual favors in return for privileges or for not being given harsher punishment in the system. Investigations have shown cases where women prisoners were coerced into receiving abortions after becoming pregnant by administrators.

Conjugal Visitation

Conjugal visitations involve a prisoner being visited by his or her spouse and being allowed spend time together privately, generally for sexual purposes. These are controversial, but are currently used by several prisons in the United States as a means of decreasing same-sex contacts among prisoners and to preserve family ties and relationships. The controversy stems from a sense that the practice is unfair to prisoners who are not married, the possibility that pregnancy may result and the prisoner will not be in a position to support the child, and from the security risks imposed by contact between a prisoner and an outsider. Further, conjugal visitations have traditionally been offered to male inmates but not female inmates, which raises an issue of fairness. Some prisons have begun allowing female inmates to have general family visitation, which can include not only conjugal visitation but visits from children.

Shock Incarceration

Shock incarceration is a relatively recent form of punishment imposed by some judges with the intent of shocking young offenders convicted of a first offense into reconsidering their behavior. These short (generally three-to-six month) periods of incarceration typically involve drug treatment and military-style training, which has led some people to refer to shock incarceration as "boot camp." The military model imposes discipline, good exercise habits, and a sense of community on young offenders. It also prevents the offenders from taking part in a prison community where they might find themselves diverted toward a criminal mentality and continued criminal behavior.

Martinson Report

The Martinson Report was produced in the late 1960s and early 1970s by researchers evaluating the effectiveness of efforts by correctional institutions to rehabilitate prisoners and prevent recidivism -- the return to criminal behavior by inmates released into the general population. Martinson's conclusion, published in 1975, was that treatment programs aimed at prisoner rehabilitation are almost always ineffective. The report created an uproar and was quite controversial. Martinson was accused of bias and of using data selectively, accusations that are quite possibly true, but his report simply verified conclusions reached by earlier, less comprehensive studies. Martinson's work encouraged attempts by others to abolish any form of rehabilitative treatment for prisoners, but also encouraged more researchers to analyze the effectiveness of these treatments, if only to refute Martinson's conclusions.

Johnson v. Avery

In the 1969 Supreme Court case Johnson v. Avery, the high court took issue with a Tennessee prison regulation that forbade prisoners to "advise, assist or otherwise contract to aid another, either with or without a fee, to prepare writs or other legal matters." The court held that the assistance of such "jailhouse lawyers," who help other prisoners with legal matters, could not be prohibited unless an alternative form of legal assistance could be provided. The case concerned a Tennessee prisoner who had repeatedly counseled other prisoners on legal matters, but who found himself placed in solitary confinement for doing so. This was the first of several Supreme Court cases that would define the rights of prisoners to give and receive legal advice.

Procunier v. Martinez

In the 1974 Supreme Court case Procunier v. Martinez, the court dealt with the issue of mail censorship by prison officials. The California Department of Corrections had placed a ban on mail that contained certain types of content, including inflammatory political views, defamatory content, or anything "otherwise inappropriate" to prisoners. The court held that this represented a violation of First Amendment rights to free speech and that censorship of prisoner mail is only justified if it "further[ed] one or more of the important and substantial governmental interests of security, order, and the rehabilitation of inmates" and " must be no greater than is necessary to further the legitimate governmental interest involved." Earlier rulings by the high court had stipulated that prison officials may search mail for contraband, but only in the presence of the prisoner and without reading the content of the mail.

Thornburgh v. Abbott

In the 1989 Supreme Court case Thornburgh v. Abbott, the high court partially reversed its own decision in the 1974 case Procunier v. Martinez, where it held that censoring prisoner mail represented a violation of First Amendment rights except under a narrow range of conditions. In Abbott, the court ruled that these conditions only applied to outgoing mail. For incoming mail, prison officials only had to establish that the reasons for censorship were reasonable. The case represented a partial return to the "hands off" policy that the court had taken toward prison mail censorship in the years prior to the 1960s.

Estelle v. Gamble

In the 1976 Supreme Court case Estelle v. Gamble, the high court dealt with the issue of giving prisoners access to medical care. J.W. Gamble, an inmate in a Texas prison, had injured his back while performing prison work. A prison doctor gave him a pass that allowed him to remain in his cell for several days of rest and ordered prison officials to allow him to sleep on an upper rather than lower bunk. Prison officials refused to comply with the latter and eventually refused to comply with the "cell pass" that allowed Gamble to remain in his cell for recuperation. The Supreme Court ruled that this had been a violation of Eighth Amendment prohibitions on the "unnecessary and wanton infliction of pain" on a prisoner. However, the Court made no specific ruling on how much medical care would be deemed adequate for prisoners in other cases.

Jones v. North Carolina Prisoners' Labor Union

In the 1977 Supreme Court case Jones v. North Carolina Prisoners' Labor Union, the high court dealt with the issue of prisoner labor unions and the right of prison inmates to engage in collective bargaining. In the 1970s, prisoners had attempted on a number of occasions to establish labor unions within their prisons for the purpose of acquiring those rights granted to state employees under labor laws. In this case, prisoners of the North Carolina Department of Corrections alleged that their right to organize had been denied by prison regulations. The high court ruled that prisons had the right to ban solicitation of prisoners by unions and to forbid the prisoners to organize as long as this does not unduly abridge free speech rights and "the regulations drafted were no broader than necessary to meet the perceived threat of group meetings and organizational activity to such order and security."

Jackson v. Bishop

The 1968 federal court ruling in the case Jackson v. Bishop concerned itself with the use of the lash as a punishment for prison inmates. At one time, flogging was a common punishment both in and out of prison, but had ceased to be a common punishment in Western society in the 20th century. In some prisons, however, it continued to be used as a punishment for inmates and was commonly used in the Arkansas prison system for violations of prison regulations. In 1968, a federal court ruled that flogging violated Eighth Amendment prohibitions against cruel and unusual punishment, in part because "corporal punishment is easily subject to abuse in the hands of the sadistic and the unscrupulous."

Wolff v. McDonnell

In the 1974 Supreme Court case Wolff v. McDonnell, the high court ruled on the applicability of due process in prisoner disciplinary proceedings. Until this ruling, the disciplining of a prison inmate was often handled in an ad hoc and informal way by various prison personnel for reasons that were capricious and frequently did not involve any form of due process. In this case, the Supreme Court laid down very specific rules for decisions on prisoner discipline and held that prisoners must be able to call witnesses in their own defense, that fact finders must present a written statement as to the purpose of the disciplinary action, and that prisoners must receive advance notice of the proceedings at least 24 hours before they begin. However, the court also ruled that prisoners have no constitutional right to cross-examination.

Rhodes v. Chapman

In the 1981 Supreme Court case Rhodes v. Chapman, the court considered the issue of "double celling" in prisons, where two prisoners share a single cell. A lower court had held that this represented a violation of the Eighth Amendment prohibition on cruel and unusual punishment because it reduced the living space available to individual prisoners. However, the Supreme Court reversed this decision, holding that while the Eighth Amendment prohibited "the wanton and unnecessary infliction of pain" and punishments that were "grossly disproportionate to the severity of the crime warranting imprisonment." However, the total circumstances under which the double celling had been imposed did not represent an unreasonable imposition on the prisoners.

Hudson v. Palmer

In the 1984 Supreme Court case Hudson v. Palmer, the high court considered the privacy rights of prisoners. Ted S. Hudson, an inmate in a Virginia prison, had been charged with destruction of state property when a guard had found a torn pillowcase in a trash can. He had been ordered to reimburse the state for the cost. He alleged that this represented "unreasonable search and seizure" and violated his constitutional rights. The high court held that the state of Virginia had reasonable grounds for searching a prisoner's belongings and living area, and that prisoners "have no legitimate expectation of privacy in their individual cells that would entitle them to Fourth Amendment protection."

Wilson v. Seiter

In the 1991 Supreme Court case Wilson v. Seiter, the high court dealt with the issue of a prisoner's right to file legal complaints about inhumane living conditions. In this case, an Ohio prison inmate named Pearly Wilson alleged that his Eighth Amendment protection from cruel and unusual punishment had been violated by the living conditions to which he had been subjected. The court ruled against Wilson, declaring that a prisoner "must show a culpable state of mind on the part of prison officials," thereby adding an intent requirement to the ban on cruel and unusual punishment. The court also held that the prison would need to demonstrate a "deliberate indifference" to the prisoner's needs before the Eighth Amendment was violated.

PRIVATIZATION OF CORRECTIONS

Privatization of corrections is the concept that prisons can be run not just by the state, but also by private organizations that undertake the operation of prisons as a profit-making venture. It is a controversial idea. In its favor, it could potentially solve problems with making prisons cost-effective, something that has been difficult for governments to do. Opponents, however, argue that it would involve a conflict of interest between the rights of prisoners and the needs of private corporations to make money from the prison's operation. For instance, there is some question as to how disciplinary measures could be handled ethically in such a situation, and there is reason to wonder whether prison owners might attempt to have sentences for certain crimes lengthened to provide an increased supply of prisoners. Nonetheless, there are now privately-run prisons in more than half of US states. The first of these was the Marion Adjustment Center in Kentucky, which opened in 1986.

COMMUNITY-BASED CORRECTIONS

Community-based corrections are activities within the local community intended to both enhance the rehabilitation of criminal offenders and to benefit in some way the community itself. In many instances, first-time offenders or those charged with minor offenses are sentenced to community service rather than prison sentences. Community service typically involves performing unpaid service for a municipality -- for instance, where that service might involve cleaning facilities or working in a homeless shelter. These services are often required of individuals convicted of a "quality of life" crime, such as vandalism and panhandling, where the community service represents a commensurate improvement of the quality of community life.

MORRISEY V. BREWER

In the 1972 Supreme Court case Morrisey v. Brewer, the court extended rights of due process to paroled convicts accused of having violated the terms of parole. In this case, parole had been revoked without a hearing. The court ruled that a hearing (now known as a Morrisey hearing) is required in all parole revocation cases. In addition, a second hearing or final hearing is required, in addition to the preliminary hearing, in order to determine what measures will be taken if it is determined that parole has been violated.

DSST Practice Test

Want to take this practice test in an online interactive format?
Check out the online resources page, which includes interactive practice questions and much more: **mometrix.com/resources719/dsstcrimjust**

1. Of the following statements, the most accurate definition of crime is

a. an act that offends society.
b. an intent to violate written laws based on natural law or accepted written standards of legal social behavior.
c. any act that inflicts physical or emotional harm on law-abiding citizens.
d. the unlawful taking, harming, or misuse of property or persons owning such property.

2. The Latin term "mens rea" refers to

a. the mental state of an individual preventing a crime.
b. the mental state of an individual intending to commit a crime.
c. the mental state of an arresting officer.
d. the mental state of an individual who commits a homicide.

3. One of the most important databases in collecting information about crime in the US is

a. the FBI's Central Bureau of Crime Collection Statistics
b. the Crime Self-Report Survey
c. the Crime Clock
d. the Uniform Crime Report

4. A key difference between the National Crime Victimization Survey and the Uniform Crime Report is that

a. The National Crime Survey collects statistics from a wider segment of the American population.
b. The Uniform Crime Report is compiled by the US Census Bureau.
c. The National Crime Report is a household survey, whereas the Uniform Crime Report derives from law enforcement agencies.
d. All of the above.

5. The "crime clock" is

a. one of the statistical readings obtained from the Uniform Crime Report.
b. one of the statistical outputs derived from the National Crime Survey.
c. a computer-based record of the frequency of crimes occurring around the world.
d. a special clock used by police departments to predict the time of the day or season of the year when certain crimes are likely to occur.

6. The crime of "date rape" refers to

a. unlawful sexual intercourse without consent and usually involving force or threat of force.
b. a rape in which an adult engages in consensual intercourse with a person below the legal age of consent.
c. consensual sexual intercourse among adults in which one of the partners later has regrets.
d. forced sexual intercourse without consent between two persons who are close friends and embarked upon a social outing.

7. Non-criminal homicide is different from manslaughter in that

a. it is usually police personnel who are involved in non-criminal homicides, while police on duty are exempt from manslaughter charges.
b. in both types of cases, the subject person does not intend to kill anyone.
c. there is no intent to kill in manslaughter, but a person may intend to kill another person in justifiable self-defense.
d. All of the above.

8. A person may be charged with burglary by entering a home

a. but only if force is used to gain entry.
b. even if the doors are unlocked and the homeowner is working in the back yard.
c. with unlocked doors, but only if the person has stolen something.
d. without authorization, and with an intent to commit a crime

9. Martha Green, 200 pounds, is jealous of Samaira Duchaines, her 90 pound rival for class president. One day Martha confronts her rival in the lavatory. During the ensuing discussion, Martha charges toward Samaira but stops short of pushing her. Martha stands face-to-face with the other girl, who is too afraid to say another word. Another student observes the incident and confirms Samaira's account that Martha threatened to "bash your head against the wall if you don't get out of my face!" Which of the following statements best applies to the situation?

a. Martha cannot be charged with assault because she did not touch Samaira.
b. Martha can be charged with assault even though she restrained herself from pushing Samaira against the wall.
c. Martha can be charged with aggravated assault, but not simple assault.
d. Martha cannot be charged with assault because she claims self-defense and that Samaira had been gossiping about her.

10. The common law derivative known as "parens patriae" has particular meaning for the juvenile justice system. The statement that best expresses what the term means in this context is:

a. Parens patriae means that the state can act as parents on behalf of and in the best interest of minor children if the court so rules.
b. Parens patriae means that parents have more legal authority than the "patriae," or country, even if both parents are in prison on felony charges.
c. Parens patriae means that the state may charge minor criminal defendants as adults but only in cases involving murder, rape, or violent assault.
d. Parens patriae guarantees that a stepparent can act in loco parentis for a juvenile accused of a crime.

11. The Constitutional Amendment which protects individual rights with regard to illegal search and seizure is the

a. Eighteenth Amendment
b. Fourth Amendment
c. Fifth Amendment
d. Sixth Amendment

12. Cesare Beccaria is best known as

a. the notorious criminal who committed Italy's largest bank heist in the 60s.
b. the first Chief of Scotland Yard.
c. the Jesuit priest who launched the first extensive campaign against capital punishment.
d. the social scientist and philosopher who founded the classical school of criminology and emphasized crime prevention over arrest and retribution.

13. Of the law enforcement organizations listed below, the organization most likely to head an investigation of state to state cigarette smuggling is

a. the Bureau of Alcohol, Tobacco, Firearms, and Explosives (ATFE).
b. the Drug Enforcement Agency (DEA).
c. the US Customs Service.
d. the Federal Bureau of Investigation (FBI).

14. The law enforcement agency most likely to be involved with moving a prisoner convicted of insider stock trading from a federal courthouse to a federal prison is

a. the FBI.
b. the Federal Securities and Exchange Commission (SEC).
c. the Secret Service.
d. the US Marshals Service.

15. Which of the following statements is false?

a. Police may legally lie to suspects when interviewing them during a criminal investigation.
b. When interviewing a complainant during an investigation of domestic abuse, police must read Miranda rights to the complainant.
c. When investigating a murder, evidence obtained in a talk with the perpetrator may not be used in court if it was illegally obtained.
d. Police may seize evidence they see on the front seat of a car while talking to the driver.

16. While responding to a complaint of domestic abuse at 123 Painful Street, the police officer is invited indoors by a battered wife. The likely suspect has fled, but the police officer inspects the bedroom and finds several bags of heroin under the mattress. The Supreme Court case that impacts the use of evidence obtained in this manner is

a. Miranda v. Arizona the.
b. The Knapp Commission v. New York City
c. Mapp v. Ohio.
d. Brown v. Board of Education.

17. The agency most likely to investigate corruption and fraud within the Social Security Administration is

a. the FBI.
b. Mollen Commission.
c. the Inspector General's office.
d. the Knapp Commission.

18. The Internal Affairs Division is

a. an offshoot of the Knapp and Mollen Commission investigations into New York City police corruption.
b. an internal local police component entrusted with investigating the conduct of its own police officers.
c. the division most likely to investigate police misconduct of its off-duty and on-duty police officers.
d. All of the above.

19. Which of the following is a weakness of Citizen Review Boards?

a. They tend to be redundant and occur after a police department's internal affairs division has already thoroughly investigated an incident.
b. They tend to be in agreement with internal police investigations.
c. They tend to be palliatives for different civilian factions, but they rarely come up with new information.
d. All of the above.

20. Which of the following is a correct statement about the difference between jails and prisons?

a. Prisons are for serious crimes, but youthful offenders are held in local jails.
b. Jails are for first-time offenders and for those who can be rehabilitated. Prisons are for prisoners who cannot be rehabilitated.
c. Jails are intended to be for prisoners who cannot make bail or who are sentenced to non-felonious crimes punishable by less than one year of incarceration. Prisons are for felons.
d. Jails are controlled by sheriff's department officers, while prisons are staffed with officers from the State Department of Corrections.

21. The three most-often performed tasks of the typical police officer are

a. patrols, investigations, and administrative tasks.
b. motor patrols, foot patrols, and detective work.
c. public relations, patrols, and community outreach.
d. All of the above.

22. Which of the following activities is not a function or purpose of police patrolling?

a. Creating a visible police presence which in itself can be a deterrent to crime.
b. Responding to initial crime complaints and gathering relevant information and evidence.
c. Using police discretion in determining an appropriate course of action with regard to illegal activity.
d. Testifying in court against an accused person.

23. In modern times—for a variety of reasons—the traditional criminal punishments of incarceration have given way to

a. house arrest, electronic monitoring, and various forms of "accelerated rehabilitation" programs for youthful and first time offenders.
b. transferring criminal offenders to military service.
c. community service sentencing and chain gangs.
d. public court apologies and seeking forgiveness from crime victims.

24. "He seemed to be the most nervous person in the crowd when I approached, so I arrested him," said the officer to the prosecuting attorney. Such an arrest would be questionable and likely to be void under the legal guidelines of

a. parens patriae.
b. probable cause.
c. nolo contendere.
d. the Fifth Amendment and self-incrimination.

25. Ahmad Jones is brought before a District Magistrate to be arraigned on charges of drunk driving. The magistrate had a nephew who was killed by a drunk driver, and she has little compassion for people who drink and drive. The defendant is found guilty and the magistrate sentences Ahmad to dig a hole in the local cemetery for another victim of a drunk driving accident. This sentence would likely be overturned due to

a. the Eighth Amendment to the US Constitution
b. the Fifth Amendment to the U.S Constitution.
c. the Fourth Amendment to the U.S Constitution
d. the Sixth Amendment

26. The Constitutional Amendment that granted equal protections under US laws to all US citizens regardless of nationality, race, or religious beliefs and has important implications for police officers is the

a. the Fifth Amendment
b. the Fourth Amendment
c. the Sixth Amendment
d. the Fourteenth Amendment

Consider the following statements to answer Question 27:

I. Female police officers are less aggressive than male officers; therefore, they are better able to control volatile situations verbally.
II. Female police officers create an officer safety problem in most police departments.
III. Female officers have a more positive attitude toward community policing than male officers do.
IV. The percentage of both male and female college graduates among police officers is much higher today than in years past.

27. With regard to gender in police hiring, which of the following statements is true?

a. I and II
b. I, III, and IV
c. III and IV
d. IV only

28. Research on police officer behavior is likely to focus on

a. use of force and the discharge of firearms.
b. detection activities, service activities, the number of arrests and citations, and the use of force.
c. the number of hours spent on patrol, firearms training, and an officer's level of education.
d. attitudes toward policing, attitudes toward the community, and attitudes toward the court system.

29. The principal elements of community policing include all of the following activities EXCEPT:

a. formal community access to police decision- and policy-making processes.
b. more police hours devoted to non-enforcement tasks such as controlling traffic, providing community services, and maintaining order.
c. being proactive in encouraging respect for authority.
d. initiating frequent personal contact with residents and members of the business community.

30. The term that applies when a juvenile court gives up jurisdiction in a criminal case to an adult court is

a. civil court jurisdictional transfer.
b. juris juvenem.
c. a waiver of jurisdiction.
d. juvenis criminem.

31. Police officers very often deal with courts of limited jurisdiction. One of the more common courts of limited jurisdiction where police officers often appear with criminal suspects is

a. a court of general jurisdiction.
b. an appeals court.
c. a justice of the peace.
d. a county court.

32. William Winchester was questioned and arrested by police officers in connection with a robbery. Mr. Winchester was later found guilty in a court of general jurisdiction. However, his defense attorneys discovered that some of the information Mr. Winchester provided to police was obtained by intense pressure law enforcement officers applied during an interview that occurred after Winchester had been told by his lawyer to remain silent. The court which would hear the case would likely be

a. an appellate court.
b. a court of limited jurisdiction.
c. a magistrate.
d. a justice of the peace.

33. Municipal or lower courts of limited jurisdiction

a. handle cases involving murder, rape, or robbery.
b. handle cases involving juvenile crime, divorce, traffic violations, and child custody.
c. handle cases in which another court has ruled and the defense attorney is appealing the verdict.
d. handle cases of police corruption.

34. The courts where cases like murder, robbery, and rape are tried are called

a. municipal or magistrate courts.
b. appellate courts.
c. courts of general jurisdiction or superior courts.
d. None of the above.

35. Which of the following is NOT a main purpose of police patrol?

a. Responding aggressively to citizen complaints and writing reports in a timely manner.
b. Maintaining contact with community residents and reassuring businesses that they are operating in a crime-free area.
c. Keeping peace in the community using outreach programs.
d. Answering calls, maintaining a crime-deterring presence, and investigating suspicious activity.

36. Two police officers are responding to a complaint of a woman claiming she has been raped. There are no physically visible signs of assault or abuse, and the complainant tells the female officer that she has dated the man who raped her. The proper course of action for the officer to follow is to:

a. write a report of the incident and tell the purported victim that it would be hard to prove rape in this case.
b. write a report of the incident and tell the purported victim she ought to make an appointment with her doctor.
c. get the purported victim to the hospital for a rape kit and write a report detailing the information obtained.
d. conduct an interview, write a report, and then take her to the hospital if her allegations make sense.

37. Sometimes new laws and court rulings have an effect opposite to the original intent. The 1961 case Mapp v. Ohio, for example, has led to "dropsy" testimony in courts. Which statement below best indicates the problem that has resulted from this case?

a. Since Mapp v. Ohio prohibits evidence illegally obtained from being used in state and federal courts, police officers have tended to ignore evidence.
b. Since Mapp v. Ohio prohibits evidence illegally obtained from being used in state and federal courts, police officers have tended to be more truthful in their statements in court.
c. Since Mapp v. Ohio prohibits evidence illegally obtained from being used in state and federal courts, police officers have tended to claim that drugs found on suspects were "dropped" and therefore are admissible as evidence in court.
d. Since Mapp v. Ohio prohibits evidence illegally obtained from being used in state and federal courts, police officers have tended to do more intense searches of criminal suspects.

38. Critics of the criminal court system often complain about "assembly line" justice. Assembly-line justice refers to

a. the secret locations where judges, prosecutors, and defense attorneys gather to plan court strategy.
b. courtrooms where judges, prosecutors, and defense attorneys meet to dispose of cases without trial.
c. plea bargains reached by all parties during the course of district court trials.
d. secret agreements between judges and defense attorneys that give defendants an advantage while freezing out prosecutors.

39. During the early days of the development of the Internet, there were no laws applying to certain activities now determined illegal by statute. This means that

a. acts committed before a law was created to make such acts illegal are not prosecutable.
b. ex post facto laws can address unethical and obviously harmful activities occurring before laws were enacted, making them prosecutable.
c. it is up to citizens in a society to know what is a crime and what is not, even if a state legislature is in the process of writing the statute.
d. ex post facto laws are constitutional.

40. The basic legal components required for something to be considered a crime are:

a. harm to society or an individual, damage to property, and an act that shows disrespect to societal norms.
b. harm to society or an individual, a statute, and a disposition to believe that a criminal act is justified.
c. a statute, a criminal intent, a criminal act, and the condition that all must occur at the same time.
d. criminal planning, a criminal idea, a statute, and the condition that all must occur at the same time.

41. An undercover police officer insinuates to a teenager that his sister, college student, will be harmed if he does not do a "favor" for the undercover officer and carry a package to the post office and mail it under his own name and return address. Because the package is found to contain a kilo of cocaine, the young man is arrested. When the facts and circumstances of the arrest come out in court, the case would likely be thrown out on the basis of illegal police procedure. The basis for the wrongful procedure is called

a. the Procedural Control Act of 1984.
b. failure to grant due process.
c. illegal search and seizure.
d. entrapment.

42. Indeterminate sentencing of convicted criminals occurs when

a. the state has set minimum and maximum lengths of sentence and a judge has the discretion to pose a sentence within those guidelines.
b. the state has set specific lengths of sentences for specific crimes so as to apply justice equally.
c. a judge may declare an amnesty for the convict after the statute minimum amount of time is served.
d. the state can proscribe a maximum sentence but the minimums are at the discretion of the judges.

43. Determinate sentences are sentences in which the criminal is given prison time and

a. the Parole Board decides the actual length of the sentence.
b. the judge has discretion to determine a lesser sentence than the one prescribed in law.
c. the prosecutor's recommendation for the length of the sentence is observed by the judge and the jury.
d. the term of the sentence is fixed by the legislature, leaving the judge no discretion in sentencing. In some states, the Parole Boards can administer earlier releases, but the points at which this may be done are also fixed.

44. States with "three-strikes laws" are those that enforce

a. life sentences for those who commit two violent felonies and even a single misdemeanor.
b. mandatory proscribed sentences in cases where an offender has committed three violent felonies.
c. long prison sentences when offenders have committed three crimes with at least one of them being a felony crime.
d. mandatory proscribed sentences in cases where an offender has committed three felonies.

45. For police departments and the law enforcement system, the universal DNA testing of arrested persons

a. can free persons wrongfully convicted of crimes.
b. can make police more efficient.
c. is currently prohibitively expensive.
d. All of the above.

46. In colonial America, most law enforcement issue were adopted from

a. Roman law.
b. Greek law.
c. religious law.
d. the mother country and other European nations.

47. Which of the following law enforcement activities is mostly likely to be subject to direct investigations by the FBI?

a. White collar crimes
b. Burglary
c. Aggravated assault
d. Drug interdiction

48. Which of the following statements is not an indication of the impact of white collar crime on American society?

a. White-collar crime erodes public confidence in financial institutions.
b. White-collar crime erodes public confidence in governmental institutions.
c. White-collar crime harms the American economy.
d. White-collar crime has little impact on capital investment in US businesses.

49. Which of the following statements best describes the illegal practice of money laundering?

a. Money laundering refers to the absence of dye-packs in bank reserve currency.
b. Money laundering means funneling illegal cash through otherwise legitimate business institutions so as to give the appearance it was legally acquired.
c. Money laundering refers to the illegal activities of drug trafficking organizations.
d. Money laundering refers to the illegal activities of corrupt politicians such as kickbacks, bribes, and extortion.

50. Which of the following is the best example of a money laundering scheme?

a. A Swiss banker who surreptitiously accepts $100,000 deposits to his bank from fictitious ABC Enterprises as a favor to his unemployed brother-in-law.
b. A large charitable contribution to a church by a man who is accused of association with known figures of the Russian Mafia.
c. The transfer of a large amount of money from a bank in California to a bank in Germany.
d. The bank deposit of $500 dollars by a street-corner hustler who obtained the money in a game of Three-Card Monte and works at a convenience store.

51. The police agency entrusted with the prosecution of cyber-attacks and technology crime is

a. the Central Intelligence Agency.
b. the Cyber Crimes and Technology Agency.
c. the FBI.
d. the Bureau of Cybercrime Investigation.

52. The 1985 Supreme Court ruling that changed police department policies on the use of deadly force was

a. Tennessee v. Garner.
b. Arizona v. Miranda.
c. the Chicago Deadly Force Ruling.
d. All of the above.

53. An unusual and questionable securities fraud case filed against an individual would be

a. first filed in a county district court, then in a state appellate court, and then in the State Supreme Court.
b. first filed in a federal district court and then in a federal appeals court, and if warranted, it would go to the US Supreme Court.
c. first filed in a lower court, then in a district court, and finally in the Supreme Court.
d. first filed in a federal court, then appealed in the State Supreme Court, and finally end in the US Supreme Court.

54. Prisons in the United States are

a. owned and operated by county, state, or federal agencies.
b. owned and operated by a combination of county, state, private, and federal agencies.
c. privately owned but operated by public agencies.
d. owned by the federal government but operated by counties and states.

55. The exponential growth of the US prison population can best be attributed to which of the following?

a. Longer prison sentences, tougher attitudes toward criminals, and increased arrests due to the drug war.
b. The growth of more serious crimes, violent television and films, and rap music.
c. More aggressive police tactics, aggressive prosecutions, and forensic DNA analysis.
d. Forensic DNA analysis, computer crime databases, and proactive crime prevention.

56. The term "total institutions" refers to

a. prisons that provide maximum security and rehabilitation services.
b. "no-frills" prisons that focus on punishment and employ behavioral methods such as the withholding of privileges to control behavior.
c. secure prisons in which inmates have very limited contact with the outside world, are constantly subject to surveillance, and live with strict regulations of all activity.
d. prisons that are entirely geared toward inmate rehabilitation.

57. Public order crimes describe a variety of behaviors that do not conform to a society's accepted standards of behavior. Select the answer choice in which all listed offenses are within the category of "public order crimes."

a. public drunkenness, disciplining a child with excessive physical force, and paraphilia.
b. prostitution, public drunkenness, and paraphilia.
c. corner drug dealing, underage drinking, and identity theft.
d. identity theft, paraphilia, and prostitution.

58. In most states, a person is considered to be "driving under the influence" or "driving while intoxicated" if his or her blood alcohol level is

a. .08.
b. .008.
c. less than .08.
d. between .008 and .08.

59. A man who runs up behind a woman walking in a public park, grabs her around the neck, and forces her to give him her purse should be charged with

a. larceny.
b. burglary.
c. robbery.
d. unlawful theft.

60. When people speak of a "broken windows model" of policing, they are referring to

a. a method of operations in which police observe no limits in the pursuit of criminals.
b. a method of police operations which aims to improve community relations.
c. a policy of police operations which calls for a response to complaints of broken windows.
d. a climate of policing in which the relationship between police and community has been fractured by continued conflict.

61. A "bench trial" for a criminal defendant means

a. the jury will be seated in three rows of benches, each occupied by four jurors.
b. a trial in which there will be no jury; instead, the judge decides the case.
c. a trial in which the judge hears the verdict of the jury but may disagree with it.
d. a trail in which the judge leads the jury into making the right decision.

62. Probation allows a criminal offender to

a. remain in the community under supervision.
b. prove that he is innocent even after conviction.
c. avoid jail time in exchange for a plea.
d. avoid prosecution by volunteering for community service.

63. Probation officers impose restrictions on criminal offenders, including

a. body and home searches without warrants.
b. a night-time return to jail after day-time employment.
c. the provision of health insurance programs.
d. severely restricted movements of the offender's family.

64. When applied to criminal prosecution proceedings, the term "intermediate sanctions" would most likely refer to

a. allowing crime victims and their families to voice their anger to criminal offenders.
b. punishments that do not result in prison time.
c. punishments that do not include probation.
d. alternative punishments that consists of fines or a combination of probation and prison time.

65. "Intermediate sanctions" can benefit the offender as well as the community. Which of the following is NOT a benefit of intermediate sanctions?

a. Intermediate sanctions are a way of reducing prison overcrowding.
b. Intermediate sanctions may impose a combination of incarceration and probation.
c. Intermediate sanctions are designed to punish rather than to rehabilitate.
d. Intermediate sanctions allow the offender to work and pay taxes.

66. Which of the following crimes is not punishable by the death penalty in the 38 states that have capital punishment?

a. Torture murder and murder for hire.
b. Murder originating in an illegal business such as drug dealing.
c. Spying and treason by a member of the US Armed Forces.
d. Incest.

67. Arguments in favor of the death penalty DO NOT INCLUDE the argument that

a. execution will help the victim and the victim's family cope with loss.
b. the death penalty does not deter criminals.
c. the death penalty is a criminal deterrent.
d. the death penalty is the only serious sentence for murdering an innocent person.

68. Opponents of the death penalty often argue that death penalty convictions may be mistakes because

a. confessions are often forced.
b. exculpatory evidence is often suppressed.
c. forensic DNA evaluation has uncovered mistaken convictions.
d. All of the above.

69. A criminal offender would be most likely to hear his or her Miranda rights

a. at the police station when he or she is processed in.
b. at the time of his or her arrest and also at the arraignment.
c. at the time of his or her arrest.
d. All of the above.

70. The word, phrase, or area that best describes the part of the law enforcement process in which a suspect is charged with a crime and asked to enter a plea is

a. an arraignment.
b. an arrest.
c. a police booking desk.
d. a magistrate's hearing.

71. An arraignment may entail all of the following actions EXCEPT

a. the criminal suspect is asked to provide his or her version of events leading to his or her arrest, and a report of this is made by the court.
b. the criminal suspect enters a plea of guilty, not-guilty, or nolo contendere.
c. the criminal suspect is informed of his or her right to have a lawyer.
d. a judge reads the charges against a criminal suspect.

Carefully read the narrative below which describes a sequence of events involving law enforcement and court adjudication and then select the best, most complete answers to Questions 72-74:

> Tarik Green is driving his new Ford Focus on Market Street in Philadelphia when he is stopped by a rookie police officer. The police officer informs Green that he was driving 46 mph in a 40 mph zone. Green tells the officer that he "may have been going 42" but no faster than that. The police officer asks Green to step out of the car and asks if he has any weapons with him. Green says that he does not, but the officer pats him down and finds two grams of powder contained in tinfoil packages. He also examines Green's wallet and finds that it contains several one hundred dollar bills.
>
> "Are you Tarik Green?" asks the police officer.
>
> "Yes, I am."
>
> "And where do you work, Mr. Green?"
>
> "Well...at the moment I'm unemployed, sir. I lost my job six months ago."
>
> "Put your hands behind your back; you're under arrest," says the policeman.
>
> The police officer radios the desk to report that he has arrested a suspect for selling illegal drugs. The officer is told to bring the suspect in, interrogate him further, and write up a report. At the police station, Green refuses to say where he obtained the tinfoil packages, so the officer continues to question him for five hours, making Green stand the entire time. Green says he will answer the question if he is allowed to make a phone call.
>
> "I hope you're not going to call a lawyer, Green, because that tells me you have something to hide," says the police officer. Then the police officer takes Green to the nearest magistrate's court on charges of selling illegal drugs. The magistrate has a particular dislike of drug dealers because they are ruining the neighborhood where she lives.
>
> "I'd advise you to plead guilty, Mr. Green, and not waste our time. How do you plead?" asks the magistrate.

Green has been in the custody of the police for hours and is very tired. He is dejected. Green thinks that if he cooperates with law enforcement, he will be released on bail. Instead, the magistrate imposes a bail of $500,000 and tells the police to take Green to the lockup.

72. Among the several problems with the criminal case described above is the fact that

a. Tarik Green's First Amendment rights were violated.
b. Tarik Green's Fifth Amendment protections against self-incrimination were not observed.
c. the magistrate set bail that was too high.
d. the police officer asked Tarik Green where he worked.

73. Another flaw in the case narrated above is that

a. Tarik Green's protections against illegal search and seizure were not observed.
b. Tarik Green was searched in violation of the Fourth Amendment.
c. there was no legitimate reason at all to search Green.
d. All of the above.

74. The arresting officer in this case made serious mistakes in

a. failing to inform Green of his Miranda rights.
b. failing to inform Green of his right to counsel.
c. failing to inform Green of his Miranda rights and of his right to defense counsel.
d. failing to get a search warrant.

75. The Harrison Act of 1914 was the

a. first major constitutional amendment to address illegal drugs.
b. first major law requiring sellers of heroine, opium, cocaine, and other drugs to be registered with the federal government.
c. first major law to require the registration of drug users.
d. first major law to require that drug offenders be rehabilitated.

76. The 1970 law that forms the basis of modern drug policy was the

a. Comprehensive Drug Abuse Prevention and Control Act.
b. Anti-drug Abuse Act.
c. Crime Control Act.
d. Violent Crime Control and Law Enforcement Act.

77. Alcohol abuse accounts for a significant increase in the occurrence of certain types of crime. Among the criminal offenses exacerbated by alcohol abuse are

a. criminal assault.
b. insider trading.
c. embezzling.
d. All of the above.

78. Which of the following may be considered a white collar crime?

a. Kidnapping
b. Illegal gambling
c. Bookmaking
d. Mail fraud

79. Mizri Smith makes cold calls to senior citizens and offers to help them reclaim a bank account held for them in the name of a deceased relative, but only if they give him such information as a social security number and date of birth. If he is caught, Smith would most likely be charged with

a. telephone fraud.
b. a white collar crime.
c. harassment.
d. identity theft.

80. Police may often encounter armed citizens in the course of duty and know there is a difference between those who are legally armed and those who are illegally armed. The body of law which forms the basis of laws applying to legally armed citizens is

a. the Miranda Case.
b. the First Amendment to the US Constitution.
c. the Second Amendment to the US Constitution.
d. the right of a militia to bear arms, as stated in English Common Law.

81. The Second Amendment right of citizens to bear arms has been upheld by the US Supreme Court but

a. applies only to law enforcement, federal police, and licensed private security agents.
b. the law applies only to militias, as the Constitution says.
c. there is still controversy about "right to carry" laws within different states.
d. applies only to revolvers, shotguns, and hunting rifles.

82. How does the US Constitutional mandate for separation of powers impact law enforcement?

a. Separation of powers has no impact on law enforcement. Police officers are independent and answer to the communities or cities in which they are hired.
b. Police are part of the executive branch, the laws are part of the legislative system, and the courts represent the judicial branch. All must operate independently.
c. Since they make decisions about crime, police departments are part of the judicial branch. The legislative branch sets standards for the judiciary branch, which tries suspected criminals. All must work together to maintain social stability.
d. Separation of powers mandates that police departments decide what constitutes a crime. The legislature sets penalties for crimes, and the courts determine guilt or innocence based on police reports and testimony.

83. A patrol officer working an early morning shift notices a car repetitively circling the parking lot of an apartment building. At 3:00 a.m., a man comes out of the apartment building and approaches the vehicle. The officer cannot hear what he and the driver are saying to each other, but the officer follows the vehicle out of the parking lot, puts on flashers, stops the vehicle, and searches it.

a. This is an illegal stop and a violation of the driver's Fourth Amendment rights against illegal search and seizure. There is insufficient reason to believe a crime has been committed. Probable cause is lacking.
b. There was no reason the car should be circling the apartment at 3:00 a.m. The man who came out of the apartment building was wearing a "hoodie" and looked suspicious. Because the officer could have been observing a drug deal, he was right to stop the vehicle and search it.
c. The officer should have gotten the vehicle's license plate number and run it though the police records checking system before stopping the vehicle and searching it. If there was a previous traffic violation on the record, the police officer would have had the right to conduct a search.
d. The officer violated the Sixth Amendment. He might have questioned the victim and determined if a crime had been committed, depending on the person's reaction to the questions.

84. One popular non-jail method of dealing with youth criminal offenders is

a. requiring that they go into the Marines or go to jail.
b. requiring that they be monitored by a cleric of their own religion.
c. requiring that they go to boot camp.
d. revoking driving privileges until age 21.

85. Common criticisms of military style boot camps are that

a. youthful offenders may be subject to abuse.
b. boot camps are less expensive than incarceration.
c. boot camps often help offenders make contact with gangs.
d. boot camps make youthful offenders have conservative political outlooks.

86. The term "recidivism" means

a. the return of severe punishment for severe offenses.
b. the tendency of car thieves to repeat the exact same type of crime when released.
c. the tendency of prison parole boards to deny parole to certain inmates.
d. the tendency of some convicted offenders to commit crimes that return them to prison after they are released for a prior offense.

87. Convicted offenders in US prison systems often differentiate between "easy time" and "hard time." Both terms refer to

a. short or long prison sentences.
b. cooperation with prison gangs.
c. the degree of ease or hardship that stems from the type of crime for which the offender is sentenced.
d. the degree of ease or hardship that may stem from conformity to the rules of the prison system and corrections officers.

88. Which of the following is not one of a prisoner's basic rights?

a. Medical care
b. Equal treatment for all races, religions, and personal beliefs
c. Protections against cruel and unusual punishments
d. A minimum two hours daily at a time of their own choosing, for meditation, prayer, or reading

89. A prison corrections officer who has had a great deal of trouble with a certain prisoner makes up stories to encourage other prisoners to assault the troublemaker. This is a violation of

a. the Eighth Amendment to the US Constitution.
b. the Fifth Amendment to the US Constitution.
c. the First Amendment to the US Constitution.
d. the Second Amendment to the US Constitution.

90. Transferring a prisoner from one institution to another prison that is 500 miles away must be legally justified because

a. prisoners must be incarcerated within 100 miles from where the closest family member lives.
b. the rights of a prisoner must always be respected.
c. transfers of criminals must not be done on a discriminatory basis.
d. some prisoners might need higher levels of security in certain prisons.

91. A police officer arrives at a scene to find a victim who was shot and killed. The officer observes that the victim has one bullet wound in the leg, and two in the upper torso. The officer notices three brass shell casings scattered within the vicinity of the body. After calling for assistance and sealing off the crime scene, the officer writes a report of his observations. The officer's report would most likely say that

a. a shotgun was used in the slaying.
b. a revolver was used in the slaying.
c. a screwdriver was used to stab the victim in three places.
d. a pistol or rifle was used in the slaying.

92. Police patrolling techniques are often described as "reactive" or "proactive." Which statement best describes the meaning of both terms?

a. A reactive patrol does not respond to a crime scene unless criminal activity is reported there. A proactive patrol establishes a strong presence in an area to prevent crimes from occurring there.
b. A proactive patrol does not respond to a crime scene unless criminal activity is reported there, while a reactive patrol tries to thwart crime by establishing a presence before crimes occur.
c. A reactive patrol is an aggressive reactor to criminal activity, whereas a proactive patrol establishes positive relationships with community residents and businesses.
d. A proactive patrol is one that conducts frequent surveillance of known criminals in the community. A reactive patrol tends to hold offenders responsible only after crimes are committed.

93. The services provided to a person who is "in forma pauperis" include

a. rehabilitative services and probation.
b. a lawyer who speaks Latin.
c. free access to courts, no court costs, and free defense counsel.
d. the entitlement to welfare benefits, which can be used to pay court costs.

94. With regard to criminal proceedings, an "indictment" is

a. the entering of a court plea by a criminal suspect.
b. a formal statement of charges against an accused as filed by the prosecuting authorities.
c. prepared by the police officers who are first summoned to respond to a crime.
d. a requirement that a suspect be read his or her Miranda rights in full view of the Court.

95. The Powell v. Alabama case refers to

a. a 1932 case in which the Scottsboro Boys were denied their right to attorneys until just prior to their trial.
b. a 1964 case in which it was established that the Scottsboro Boys were subject to cruel and unusual punishment.
c. a 1964 case in which the Scottsboro Boys were exonerated because they were tried without having defense counsels present.
d. a 1930 case in which several young Alabama men were accused of capital murder.

96. The term "pre-trial diversion" refers to

a. a judicial instruction to the jury in a criminal case.
b. diverting a criminal suspect from pleading innocent by offering that person incentives to plead guilty.
c. a pre-trial conference between prosecutors and defense attorneys to agree on the length of a prison term.
d. the practice of diverting minor offenders away from traditional punishments and imprisonments.

97. The "innocent until proven guilty" concept has practical meaning for some criminal suspects. Which of the following is an advantage that a criminal may gain from being innocent until proven guilty?

a. A suspect may be released on his or her own recognizance.
b. A suspect may be deemed "in former pauperis."
c. A suspect may be granted the right to a fair trial.
d. A court may impose a bail so high that it is impossible for the suspect to return home.

98. A criminal defense lawyer files a pre-trial discovery motion. This means that

a. the lawyer is demanding that his client be released from jail at once.
b. some of the prosecution evidence can be thrown out of court.
c. the lawyer is requesting that all prosecution evidence be turned over to the defense.
d. the lawyer has discovered evidence that proves his client is innocent and wants to present it to the court.

99. Preventive detention may be employed

a. only in rare cases where a suspect can be held without charges because of the high likelihood of injury or death to others.
b. in cases where suspected terrorists are known to be planning attacks.
c. in cases where mentally ill people have previously killed, are likely to kill others, and have been legally judged to be dangerous.
d. All of the above.

100. A "warrantless search"

a. will always be thrown out of court.
b. is always determined to be a legal search in auto stops and frisks.
c. is one that a police chief authorizes to determine that a search is legal.
d. refers to one of the many conditions which are exceptions to the Fourth Amendment protections against illegal search and seizure.

Answer Key and Explanations

1. B: The best answer should take into account the basis of law, which is that laws are based upon fundamental conceptions of morality. Such fundamental conceptions are often termed "natural law." Another fundamental conception is that of "social deviance," but it is important to remember that social deviance can vary from one society to another, as do the laws in different states, countries, or communities. Choice "b" is the best answer. Keep in mind that there may be an "act which offends society" without committing a crime, that there are crimes which do not involve "physical or emotional harm," and that all crimes are not property-related.

2. B: It is important to recognize that there is such a thing as justifiable homicide, often in cases of self-defense. The person who commits justifiable homicide does not have a guilty mind and does not intend to commit the act. "Mens rea" refers to the state of mind of a person who knows an act is illegal but commits the act anyway. The term literally means "guilty mind." Choice "b" is the best answer.

3. D: Be careful of questions designed to trick you. Choice "a" does not exist; it is a made up entity. The "crime clock" and the crime "self-report survey" are actual resources; however, these are not the best answers because those terms are simply part of the two main databases used in collection of criminal statistics. The correct answer is "d," the Uniform Crime Report. The other major database used in crime collection statistics is the National Crime Victimization Survey.

4. C: The National Crime report derives from actual reports from police agencies across the country. It is more reliable than the National Crime Survey, which is compiled from a limited number of households. Self-reporting is not always accurate, and there are other limitations in the methodology employed, thereby leaving the National Crime Survey questionable in terms of accuracy. Choice "c" is the best answer. Choices "a" and "b" are simply not true, which makes "d" a wrong answer as well.

5. A: It would be nice if there were an instrument that could be used by police departments to predict when crimes would occur, but "d" will never be a reality. "C" is incorrect as well because both reports are national, not international. The correct answer is "a;" the crime clock is a statistical representation indicating the frequency of crimes. For example, the crime clock might measure the number of domestic abuse reports per minute in the US

6. D: A key point to remember in determining rape is whether or not consent is given. In "date rape," consent is particularly important in that sexual activity may have occurred among friends or acquaintances during agreeable social activity. Choice "a" refers to "forcible rape;" choice "b" refers to "statutory rape;" choice "c" does not constitute rape merely because one person has "regrets" about a consensual encounter. Answer "d" is the correct one—note that the phrase "without consent" is a key concept.

7. C: Manslaughter charges can derive from accidents or physical confrontations, but the charge is warranted only in those cases where there is clearly no intent to kill another. Non-criminal homicide can be legitimately claimed by a person who grabs a gun and intends to kill a knife-wielding home invader in self-defense and does so. That difference is best expressed in "c" but, of course, much depends on the circumstances determined in the course of a thorough police investigation. Choice "a" is wrong; police are not exempt from manslaughter if they cause the death of another person, even if the act is not intentional.

8. D: Burglary can be a tricky subject. It doesn't matter whether the doors are locked or unlocked or whether the homeowner is home or not. The key issue is that the burglar unlawfully enters a home or a business with intent to commit a crime. Without authorization from the proprietor and with the purpose of committing a crime, the intruder can be charged with burglary. Of course, the issue of intending to commit a crime can be argued by criminal attorneys and the prosecutor. Choice "d" is the best answer. Force is not required for this charge, and the burglar may be unsuccessful even though he has the intent.

9. B: The threat of bodily harm and the capability of causing harm are sufficient to merit a charge of assault against Martha, even though she restrained herself from physical contact. The best answer is "b." Unless she held a gun or knife to Samaira's head or did bang her into the wall, Martha would not likely be charged with "aggravated assault," the more serious charge that is a felony. Martha's physical capabilities would come into consideration in terms of her ability to harm Samaira and, therefore, would be a factor in an assault charge.

10. A: Latin terms can often be troubling, but in this case, a literal translation will help you get the right answer. The term literally means the "country as parents." Another way of saying that is that the state (being the "country") can serve as the parents in cases where the court has so ruled that other parental options are not in the best interest of the minor. Choice "a" is the only accurate answer to the question; the other answer choices are incorrect.

11. B: The Fourth Amendment protects individual rights with regard to illegal search and seizure. It also requires that investigating authorities show probable cause to a judge before a legal search warrant may be obtained. Although the Fifth Amendment protects individual rights against self-incrimination, it contains no protections against illegal searches. The Eighteenth Amendment has nothing to do with individual protections because it pertains to alcohol prohibition. The Sixth Amendment states that defendants in criminal cases have the right to a speedy trial.

12. D: Though it is true that Cesare Beccaria was Italian and had been educated in a Jesuit school, but he was not a priest. He was not a criminal, nor was he Chief of Scotland Yard, as answer choices a, b, and c suggest. He did write a treatise against capital punishment, but that was just one small part of his life's work in criminology. The correct answer is "d;" Beccaria introduced humane notions to criminal proceedings, emphasizing reform in many areas of criminal law and methodology.

13. A: The clue to be found in the question itself is in the phrase "state to state." While US Customs may be involved in investigations of cigarette smuggling, Customs would typically investigate smuggling in and out of US national borders. The DEA and FBI are not the main law enforcement agencies for this type of crime. The ATFE is most likely to be involved in interstate cigarette smuggling to avoid taxes. The best answer is "a."

14. D: The SEC is a federal entity, and though it does regulate securities trading, it does not transport prisoners. This particular law enforcement responsibility goes to the US Marshals Service. The US Marshals service also enforces orders and rulings of the federal courts, as in the court-ordered integration of southern schools many decades ago. The US Marshals Service may also be ordered to provide protection to witnesses in federal cases, including those who are relocated because of incriminating testimony.

15. B: The false statement is "b." Police may speak with complainants or possible suspects until and/or unless it becomes certain that an arrest must be made based on observations or other factors. If an arrest is made, the suspect must be immediately read his or her Miranda rights. The remaining statements are all true. Police officers should be especially careful with suspects who exercise their Miranda rights by requesting an attorney and then continuing to talk without the attorney present. Any information obtained in this manner becomes of little use to the prosecution in court.

16. C: Rule out "d" right away, as that well-known decision was a landmark in desegregation legislation and therefore has nothing to do with evidence. Miranda v. Arizona, which stated that a likely suspect must be read his or her Miranda rights before a police officer can obtain such evidence, does not apply in this situation, and the explanation that Miranda rights must be read before "obtaining such evidence" is intentionally misleading. The Knapp Commission investigated police corruption in New York City. In 1961, the Supreme Court ruled that evidence obtained without a legal search warrant must be withheld from prosecution in Mapp vs. Ohio, answer choice "c."

17. C: It is important to know that each federal agency has its own investigatory arm and that authority resides in the departmental Inspector General's office. Both the Knapp and Mollen Commissions investigated police corruption in New York City, but those investigations are well in the past, a fact that makes these answer choices wrong. The FBI might assist in some types of fraud investigations, particularly those involving money laundering, but the primary responsibility for investigating Social Security corruption and fraud lies with the Inspector General's office, answer choice "c."

18. D: Most police departments have internal affairs officers and sometimes even a whole department, depending on the size of the police agency. The Knapp and Mollen Commissions shocked the public by revealing the extent of police corruption; these commissions led to the establishment of many internal affairs divisions among police departments. Internal Affairs can also investigate the conduct of off-duty officers based on the assumption that corruption oftentimes spills over into off-duty activities.

19. D: Citizen Review Boards are typically favored by activist citizens who feel that their police departments need civilian control. While Civilian Review Boards provide a political advantage in terms of police partnerships with communities, statistics show that most Civilian Review Boards come to the same conclusions as internal affairs departments. Of course, citizen activists have a right to participate in community policing if they wish, and that right must be respected, so long as the work of review boards does not interfere with police work.

20. C: This is a question which requires the best answer. A little bit of knowledge will not help you here because there is a bit of truth in all answer choices. Eliminate answer "b" because the phrase "cannot be rehabilitated" is wrong. Choice "a" is tempting; however, youthful offenders often commit serious crimes, and one may successfully argue that all crimes are serious. Rule out "d" because the staffing of prisons and jails is not an indication of their purposes and may vary from state to state. Choice "c" is the best answer. "Felon" should tip you off that the offense earns a criminal more than one year in prison.

21. A: Studies of the time spent by the average police office indicate that patrols, investigation, and administrative tasks occupy the largest part of a police officer's time. Some police officers are averse to paperwork and other administrative tasks, but well-organized and well-documented paperwork aids in the prosecution of criminal offenses. All of the elements are important, but "a" is the best answer.

22. D: Police are often sent to patrol specific areas for specific reasons. Patrols may be focused on known "trouble spots," for example. In such case, the visible presence of a police officer can help curtail criminal activity. Should crimes occur, patrolling police may investigate to obtain vital information. Police must use discretion in determining the proper course of action to follow based on the evidence that has been gathered. "D" is the correct answer; giving testimony as a court witness is sometimes a result of patrolling, but it is never the purpose of a patrol.

23. A: Option "c" is half right, but "chain gangs" are no longer part of the penal system. There was a time when criminal offenders were offered the chance to serve in the military instead of serving a prison sentence, but today's military does not want criminals in its ranks, making answer "b" a poor choice. While public apologies seem to be in vogue, they are an irrelevant part of the punishment system. The best answer is "a."

24. B: A police officer needs "probable cause" to arrest someone; just because someone looked like "the most nervous person in the crowd" is not probable cause. Even if other evidence turns up later against that same person, the police are very likely to be judged to have made a "false arrest" when the defense attorney raises objections as to the reasons for the arrest.

25. A: There are certain constitutional amendments which particularly impact upon criminal procedure and it behooves every police officer to be familiar with them. The Eighth Amendment protects citizens from "cruel and unusual punishment" that the magistrate has ordered. The Sixth Amendment has to do with rights to a speedy and fair trial, the Fifth with protections against self-incrimination, and the Fourth with illegal search and seizure.

26. D: The Fourteenth Amendment dates back to the period following the Civil War when it was necessary to guarantee to African Americans the same legal protections that applied to Caucasians. The Fourteenth Amendment provides these guarantees in matters of criminal procedure. Choice "d" is the correct answer, and it is important to note that respect for the civil liberties of all citizens is an important aspect of police power and authority.

27. C: An existing study shows that the number of college graduates among police officers has risen from 20 percent in the 1960s to 65 percent in 1988. With regard to I and II, it should not surprise you that statistics show that the slight differences between male and female officers are not statistically significant. However, female officers are shown in studies to have a more positive attitude toward community policing than do their male counterparts.

28. B: All police department require high standards of hygiene and conduct so that's not likely to be a large research area. The number of hours spent on patrol might be studied locally but it's not an issue of national concern. Attitudes are important but studies show that the attitudes mentioned here affect police efficacy only slightly. The best answer is "b." Detection activities, service activities, the number of arrests and citations, and the use of force are the areas most often studied in research on police conduct and behavior.

29. C: Community policing means that the police and the community must work together to create conditions that support public safety and provide a secure environment for all citizens. The community may participate in the oversight of police policies and activities. Police officers may serve in public schools or foster drug prevention or athletic programs among community youth. All of these activities help to maintain order. The answer option that is not true is "c." Police are more apt to get respect from the community by serving in it a variety of ways rather than by demanding respect.

30. C: When a defendant is a juvenile, the juvenile court has first authority in that case, and it cannot be remanded to adult court without a "waiver of jurisdiction." The other choices are meant to mislead, and your best protection against being misled is to familiarize yourself with "waivers of jurisdiction." Although they appear to be Latin phrases concerning juvenile crime, "juvenis criminem" and "juris juvenem" are made-up phrases. The key to eliminating "a" as an answer is the phrase "civil court" because the question here refers to criminal court matters.

31. C: A police officer must recognize that different courts have different jurisdictions and different levels of authority. It is possible that a police officer will be called upon to provide testimony in just about any court, but it is highly likely that every police officer will appear most frequently in the lower courts. The Justice of the Peace, or Magistrate's Court, is one of the lowest courts of limited jurisdiction. The correct answer is "c." Another example of a lower jurisdictional court is family and juvenile court.

32. A: Police officers know that due process rights include the right to appeal decisions made by the lower courts. For this reason, most police officers are careful about following proper police procedures so as not to abrogate civil rights of individuals. Failure to observe due process often lands a case in an appellate court, where appeals of earlier decisions are held.

33. B: Routine police work often requires routine visits to the lower courts for traffic offenses, drunk and disorderly conduct, and juvenile crime. Other types of cases in the lower court category may involve wills and estates, divorce, child custody and a variety of what are generally considered minor offenses. Lower courts do not have jurisdiction for murder, rape, kidnapping, bank fraud, robbery, and other felony crimes. Being lower courts, they do not rule on appeals or police corruption.

34. C: Sometimes the terminology applied to courts can be daunting, but there is no reason to be confused. Courts of general jurisdiction are in the middle of the court process and deal with serious crimes. You may already know that courts of general jurisdiction are sometimes referred to as "superior courts." "C" is the correct answer. Do not let the word "superior" influence you into thinking that appeals go there. Most cases are appealed in special courts called "appellate courts." The highest appellate court in any state is the state supreme court.

35. A: Answer choices "b," "c," and "d" are all important purposes of police patrol. Answer choice "a" can be ruled out because responding "aggressively" is not always the best path to follow when complaints are investigated, especially since an intimidating police presence is oftentimes counter-productive. Furthermore, while writing reports in a timely manner is a duty of police officers, doing so is not a purpose of police control.

36. C: Any claim of rape must be taken seriously even if there are no physically visible signs of assault and regardless of whether the purported victim knows her assailant. It is most important to immediately get the complainant to a doctor for an examination and administration of a rape kit. Police officers must include detailed information of the complainant's allegation in their report. It is not up to responding officers to determine whether the allegations "make sense," nor should they make judgments about the difficulty of proving rape, as suggested in answer "a." Choice "c" is the only answer in this instance.

37. C: More intense searches of suspects is not a result of Mapps v. Ohio, so "d" is not the right answer. Moreover, statistics would show that there are more incidents of policy perjury after the Mapp vs. Ohio court ruling, a finding that eliminates answer choice "b." It is more rare for police to "ignore" evidence as suggested in answer choice "a" than it is for police to lie and say that a suspect dropped the drugs so that this kind of information could be used in court.

38. B: Assembly line justice refers to courtroom work groups which dispose of cases without the expense of a trial. Participants include the judge, the defense, and the prosecution. The purpose of these workgroups is to save money and time and to dispose of generally lower-category crimes and misdemeanors. The defendants are presumed to be guilty, and the chief issues of the case then become the penalties to be levied. The best answer is "b" because the key issue in assembly line justice is to avoid trial.

39. A: To answer this question, it is important to read each statement carefully and to know that "ex post facto" laws are unconstitutional. Unless a statute or law is written, it is not a crime nor prosecutable as such. "A" is the correct answer even though the first part of the statement in "b" is true. But such ex post facto laws cannot be prosecuted, eliminating that as a possible answer. "C" can be ruled out because being in the process of writing a law is not the same as having one used as a basis for prosecution.

40. C: A basic approach to solving this question is to find weaknesses in each statement that can exclude the statement as an answer choice. There must be a law against something, certainly, but it is not illegal if a person has a criminal idea and plans it at the same time. (That person might be a novelist, for instance.) Also, one may consider "harm to society or an individual" or "disrespect for societal norms" to be the result of something as un-criminal as gossip or satire. That leaves choice "c" as the correct answer.

41. D: It is illegal for a police officer to ensnare a suspect who has no intent of committing a crime without the idea of the crime being put into his or her head by the police. The naiveté of the teenager in failing to determine that his sister is, in fact, safe at college is not sufficient to establish that he wanted to be a drug dealer. Answer "a" is not a real act. Answer "c" is not logical the situation does not involve an issue of illegal search and seizure. There would be an issue of due process, but before that could occur, the case would be thrown out because it constitutes illegal police entrapment, option "d."

42. A: Indeterminate sentencing means that the minimum and maximum sentences are written into law and a judge has discretion in sentencing within those parameters. Indeterminate sentencing is believed to provide an incentive for a convict to be rehabilitated. In states that have indeterminate sentencing, parole boards have a greater role in that they can adhere to the minimum sentence proscribed in the guidelines. In other words, a convict with a two-year sentence can be released on probation at any minimum sentence length—18 months, for example.

43. D: Judges can order convicts to prison time; however, with determinate sentencing, the period is fixed by statute or law. A judge has no discretion to levy a lighter sentence. In states where the Parole Board can recommend a shorter sentence, the shorter sentencing periods are also fixed. Determinate sentencing statutes adopted by various states grew from the concern that dangerous criminals were being released too soon into the communities. Answer "d" is the best answer.

44. D: Paying attention to small details is important in answering this question correctly. The key word is "felony." It does not matter if the felonies are non-violent; states with three-strikes laws still have mandatory sentences for three-strike violators, even if one or two of the offenses are non-violent crimes. The correct answer is "d." Misdemeanors do not count, so "a" can be eliminated; "b" is not a consideration for reasons already stated; and "c" is not correct because all three strikes must be a type of felony.

45. D: The well-known attorney Barry Scheck, who heads the national DNA Project, believes that DNA sampling should be used only to clear persons wrongfully convicted because the sampling process is expensive and time consuming. On the other hand, DNA can be taken from saliva and can make police more efficient in capturing perpetrators of such crimes as rape and murder. All of the assertions are correct, so the correct answer is "d."

46. D: All of the answer possibilities have some validity in that law enforcement and justice administration is a fluid, frequently changing body of thought. The Romans, for example, borrowed from the Greeks and other older civilizations, transforming customs and religious practices into law. By the time of America's law had developed into the decentralized system it remains today, there were concepts of justice that were drawn from ancient civilizations and from religions, but America's colonial police systems came most directly from Britain (sometimes termed the "mother country") and other European nations. The best answer is "d."

47. A: Burglary and aggravated assault are typically handled by local police departments and tried in local district courts. The Drug Enforcement Agency is the enforcement arm that is involved most directly with drug interdiction, though it is important to keep in mind that any law enforcement agency may request FBI assistance if warranted by exceptional circumstances. However, the best answer is "a;" so called "white collar" crimes involve securities and health care fraud and similar crimes.

48. D: In order for society to function effectively, people must be confident of their institutions, both financial and governmental. When people feel that their institutions are fraudulent and corrupt, they are less likely to invest in the economy. Answer option "d" states that white-collar crime has little impact on capital investment, which is an untrue statement. The US economy requires capital injection to expand, and that means people must be willing to put money into banks, stocks, or other entities that fund business operations.

49. B: While drug trafficking organizations frequently engage in money laundering enterprises, money laundering is a criminal act that may involve any type of organization, even legal ones. Money laundering is the practice of disguising the illegal origins of money and making it appear to have been earned or given by other sources. Churches, banks, businesses—any enterprise may engage in the practice if there is a desire to profit from the criminal act. "B" is the best answer.

50. A: Again, we are looking for the best answer which, in this case, means the one mostly likely to be a clear case of money laundering. The definition requires that the money be illegally obtained. That would qualify the street-level hustler, but that money could have come from his job at the convenience store, as well as from the illegal gambling hustle. Choice "b" can be eliminated because that man may be a legitimate businessman who unknowingly sat next to a member of the Russian Mafia in a restaurant. Choice "c" is a common type of legal transaction. The best choice is "a" because the man has no known means of obtaining the money except through illegal means, while the banker "surreptitiously" hides the money from a "fictitious" enterprise or business.

51. C: The CIA is actually prohibited from most operations on US soil and would enlist the aid of the FBI in any investigation of domestic cyber-crime originating overseas. The Federal Bureau of Investigations handles all complaints and investigations involving technology theft, hacking, and cyber attacks. Choices "b" and "d" are fictitious entities.

52. A: Police policy on the use of deadly force is subject to the Tennessee v. Garner ruling in 1985. The Tennessee v. Garner ruling revised the previous policy allowing police to use deadly force to stop a fleeing felon. The ruling expanded the policy to require that police could use deadly force only when a suspect posed a significant threat of death or serious injury to the police officer or to others. Local police departments and agencies responded to the court ruling by adapting their own policies around the ruling.

53. B: Essentially, there are two separate court systems in the United States, but many types of different courts may exist within these peripheries. Although some crimes are violations of both state and federal laws, the systems may generally be considered separate entities. A violation of federal law, such as in securities fraud, would be first filed in the federal district court, then moved to a federal appeals court, and finally reviewed by the US Supreme Court.

54. B: The growth of private prison corporations is a relatively recent phenomenon. The Corrections Corporation of America is one of the largest and best-known, owning and operating about 34 prisons. In addition to these, Corrections Corporation of America operates more than 40 other prisons that are owned by states, counties, or federal entities. Counties, states, and the federal government own the largest part of the prison system, so we can say that prisons may be owned by state, federal, county, or private operators. Therefore, "b" is the best answer.

55. A: All of the answer options have an impact on criminal prosecution and imprisonment, but the question asks for the "best." The factors indicated in answer "a" are the ones best supported by a preponderance of statistical data. Because the use of DNA in police forensics has resulted in both convictions and exonerations, it has not had a significant overall impact on the prison population. Violent television, film, and rap music cannot be blamed for the steep increase in prison populations. The drug war, mandatory sentencing policies, and tougher attitudes toward criminal offenders have accounted for most of the increase.

56. C: The term "total institution" refers to a prison with extensive security provisions that maintains constant control over individual inmates. Prisoners are isolated from the outside world and forced to follow strict rules and regulations. Rule violations lead to additional punishment or segregation from other prisoners

57. B: Police officers may encounter paraphiliacs during a duty shift so it is important to have some idea what paraphilia is in order to answer this question correctly. Paraphilia is a complex psychiatric disorder that manifests as deviant sexual behavior. Paraphilia may take a variety of forms, including pedophilia, nymphomania, and exhibitionism, and most police officers have heard of the "Peeping Tom," a paraphiliac who depends on voyeurism to achieve sexual arousal. Paraphilia is indeed a public order crime, as are drug or alcohol offenses, prostitution, and underage drinking. Identity theft and child abuse fall into other categories of crime, so "b" is the right answer to this question. A characteristic that defines a crime as a public order crime is that many of these crimes may not have been illegal in some societies at certain periods; for instance, cocaine was once legal in the United States.

58. A: This is one answer any police officer should know. All 50 states set blood alcohol levels which define drunk driving. Most states define it as .08 percent, though others set it a bit higher at .10 percent. In some states, police can immediately seize a person's driver's license during an arrest for drunken driving. Some states that take away driving privileges make exceptions for offenders, but only to drive back and forth to work. Other states allow no driving during the entire period for which the driving license has been suspended.

59. C: This crime is certainly unlawful and it is theft, but you are to pick the best answer. You are expected to know the difference between larceny, burglary, and robbery in order to answer this question. The crime of taking with force or threat of force is "robbery." Larceny differs from robbery in that neither force nor threat of force is employed to commit the crime. Examples of larceny include pick-pocketing or purse-snatching. Burglary pertains to theft from a home or business. The correct answer is "c" because the perpetrator uses force and fear to commit the crime.

60. B: The "broken windows model" of policing refers to police operations that place great emphasis on community relations. Adherents to this policy believe it is important for police to gain the confidence of the community by responding to its needs. The concept grew from a widely-noticed article in *Atlantic Monthly* magazine entitled "Broken Windows." The article challenged the traditional crime-fighting role of police and advocated focusing police attention on a wide array of social disorders.

61. B: There are instances where a criminal defendant might decide to waive his or her right to trial by a jury of peers. In such cases, the verdict will be delivered by the judge after the opposing lawyers have presented their arguments. In other words, the verdict comes "from the bench." A bench trial is common in cases where the defendant acknowledges a level of guilt and, in return for saving the taxpayers the time and expense of a trial, enters into a plea arrangement. It may also occur in a "rehabilitative" case involving a minor crime and a first time offender.

62. A: Probation used to be the only way criminal offenders could avoid jail time. Probation allows an offender to remain in the community under supervision. The supervision can include unannounced visits by probation officers, telephone contacts, urine testing, and electronic monitoring. Choice "a" is the best answer. Choices "b," "c," and "d" are not feasible options.

63. A: Probation officers can impose a variety of restrictions upon an offender in order to enhance monitoring capability, but they have no right to impose restrictions on the offender's family, as indicated in answer choice "d." While there are programs that allow offenders to leave jail and go to work, these are not part of a person's probation, which makes answer choice "b" invalid. Health insurance programs, answer "c," are not handled by county probation offices. The correct answer is "a;" unannounced visits and searches are allowed under probationary rules.

64. D: Intermediate sanctions range from probation to prison time but do not include capital punishment or life sentences. A judge may sentence an offender to a term in jail and also the time at which he/she may be eligible for probation. Choice "b" is not the right answer, nor is "c," because intermediate sanctions may entail both jail time and probation. Choice "a" has nothing to do with intermediate sanctions.

65. C: Intermediate sanctions were a development of the 1990s, primarily in response to the problem of overcrowded prisons. A basic premise of intermediate sanctions is that criminal offenders should work, make restitution for their crimes, and pay taxes. Intermediate sanctions may consist of both incarceration and probation. Choice "c" cannot be considered a benefit of intermediate sanctions because the basic purpose of intermediate sanctions is inclined more toward rehabilitation than punishment. Therefore, the "c" is the correct answer to the question.

66. D: Incest is a horrible crime that causes extensive damage to the victims, but the death penalty is not applied in incest cases unless the crime has been compounded by other circumstances, such as the ones described in "a," "b," or "c." You should keep in mind the fact that military death sentences are imposed in military courts, which have somewhat different rules than civilian courts.

67. B: Proponents of the death penalty often argue that life sentences in modern jails are not severe enough punishments for criminals who have murdered innocent people. Supporters of capital punishment also believe that the death penalty deters other would-be criminals and that a victim's family will find peace in the serious retribution the death penalty exacts. Answer "b" is the one argument that death penalty supporters do not make and so is the right answer here.

68. D: Most people involved in law enforcement and justice administration have heard all of these arguments. Noted attorney Barry Scheck founded the DNA project which has resulted in the release of some convicts on death row. Defense lawyers routinely argue that police departments sometimes force confessions, and that exculpatory evidence has either been hidden or suppressed by police and prosecutors. All of these arguments are typically heard in death penalty cases, and these must be assiduously evaluated on their own merits.

69. B: If the justice administration process is working properly, a criminal offender will hear his or her Miranda rights at the time of his or her arrest and also at the time of arraignment. There is good reason for twice informing criminal suspects of their Miranda rights. One reason is that defense lawyers frequently claim that police failed to "Mirandize" their clients, thus making the suspect's remarks to police inadmissible as evidence. Another reason is that the judge can make sure the suspect understands his or her Miranda rights. Answer choice "b" is the best answer.

70. A: Criminal charges are typically made against a criminal suspect in a magisterial, district, or federal court. The process of a suspect's court appearance to hear the charges and to be informed of his or her rights is called an "arraignment." The reason formal charges are not read at the time of the arrest or during the booking process is that the court or prosecutors may file additional charges. The police investigate and file reports, which are then used as a basis for the charges. A hearing in a magistrate's court is not the proper term to use for a criminal arraignment.

71. A: The purpose of an arraignment is to enter a plea, to inform the suspect of his or her rights, and to hear the charges. At times during an arraignment hearing, however, a criminal suspect will attempt to convey to all attending parties that an injustice has been done. The criminal suspect may try to tell a version of events that differs from the version upon which the charge(s) is/are based. However, an arraignment is not the place for this, and a suspect who tries during an arraignment to provide his or her version of events leading to the arrest will be stopped.

72. C: Although there are many problems in the narrative that could result in having the case thrown out of court, the police officer is allowed to ask Mr. Green where he works. Green's First and Fifth Amendments have not been violated in this scenario. However, the bail of $500,000 is too high and is a violation of the Eighth Amendment because the amount is well beyond the seriousness of the "crime."

73. D: Choice "d" is the best answer to this question. The Fourth Amendment protects against illegal search and seizure. The police officer had stopped Green for a routine traffic violation; unless the suspected powder was plainly visible, there was no reason for the officer to go into Green's pockets to seize it. A police officer could have searched Green if he had been observed selling or buying drugs previously or if there had been a tip from a reliable informant who knew of Green's illegal drug activity.

74. C: The directions are that you are to pick the best, most complete answer. Choices "a" and "b" are both correct, but they are incomplete. The complete and correct answer is "c." The prospect of getting a search warrant may legitimately cross a person's mind in pointing out the failures of procedure in this case, but this is also an incorrect answer. In order for a search warrant to be issued, the police officer would have had to take the matter before an appropriate judge, and "probable cause" would have to be established. In this case, there were no evident signs of illegal activity that would have allowed for the "probable cause" necessary for a search warrant and a legal search.

75. B: The Harrison Act of 1914 was not a constitutional amendment; it was an act of Congress that called for the regulation of certain drugs and the registration of entities selling these drugs or derivatives of these drugs. The Harrison Act did not require registration of "drug users" as suggested in answer "c," nor did it have anything to do with rehabilitation. Prior to the Harrison Act of 1914, there were no federal laws prohibiting the sale of drugs termed dangerous and addictive.

76. A: The criminal justice student should have a good general idea of the evolution of legislation impacting policies regarding illegally sold drugs. The first major law regulating drug sales was the Harrison Act of 1914. The Comprehensive Drug Abuse Prevention and Control Act was passed in the 1970s and served as the basis for subsequent laws such as the Crime Control Act and the Violent Crime Control and Law Enforcement Act, both of which enhanced enforcement and prosecution of illegal drug activity.

77. A: While one could make the argument that alcohol abuse lowers inhibitions (which it does) and leads to many other types of crime, answer choices "c" and "d" can be ruled out because they are not illegal activities that can be directly attributed to alcohol abuse. The best answer is "a," criminal assault.

78. D: "White collar crime" is a term coined in 1939 by Professor Edwin Sutherland. Sutherland defined white collar crime as a "crime committed b a person of respectability and high social status in the course of his occupation." Today, the term generally refers to a variety of nonviolent frauds usually committed by business or government officials seeking monetary gain. Bookmaking and illegal gambling are not the types of crimes that fall within the definition of "white collar crime." Kidnapping is a felony offense, not a white collar crime. The best answer is "d." Mail fraud is often conducted by white collar criminals.

79. D: Although the senior citizens being contacted may feel harassed by Smith's phone calls, criminal harassment is a specific type of charge, which makes answer choice "c" not the correct one. Smith may also be a "white collar criminal" who uses the telephone to commit fraud, but he is specifically trying to get social security account numbers, dates of birth, and other personal data, which makes him guilty of identity theft. Identity theft is on the rise in this increasingly technological age. Answer choice "d" is the correct one.

80. C: Miranda refers to a suspect's legal protections against self-informing and rights to have a counsel present during questioning. The First Amendment is often referred to as the "free speech" amendment, though it encompasses other rights, too. English common law has little to do with the right of citizens to bear arms. However, the US Constitution does have a great impact on state laws governing the use of firearms. The basis of these laws is the Second Amendment to the US Constitution; answer "c" is correct.

81. C: As a police officer or criminal justice administrator, you will become familiar with firearms to one extent or another, so it is important to know the laws that are pertinent in the state where you work. The US Supreme Court has decided that the Second Amendment applies across the entire country, but nearly all states and localities are still impose restrictions, making the right to bear arms an area of considerable controversy. Answer choice "c" is correct. Choices "d" and "a" are wrong because legally armed private citizens may possess and carry semi-automatic weapons for self-defense purposes. While the "militia" referred to in answer choice "b" is mentioned also in the wording of the Second Amendment phrasing, it has been interpreted by the Supreme Court to extend to private citizens.

82. B: Except for choice "b," all answers are either incomplete or misleading. Separation of powers does impact law enforcement, and the Constitution deems it highly important that all branches be independent of each other. There must be no collusion with those who execute or act upon the laws created by the legislature. Courts, too, must examine evidence independently; they are not an extension of the legislative branch or the police departments operating under the executive branch of government.

83. A: The Fourth Amendment protects citizens against illegal search and seizure. There must be evidence or probable cause that a crime has been committed before an officer can conduct a search. Police officers cannot act upon suspicion alone, and there was no reason to think that a drug deal was taking place. Within the narrative, there could be dozens of good and legitimate reasons the events described would be legitimate and legal, making what went on a protected, private matter.

84. C: The placement of youth offenders in "boot camps" is a common recommendation of juvenile courts. Boot camps for juvenile offenders are modeled after military boot camps and attempt to teach discipline, respect for authority, and sometimes job training. In most case, courts would not revoke a youth's driving privileges because that impedes those rehabilitative plans that require offenders to be employed. It is a cleric's job to monitor youth offenders, as suggested in "b." In the past, judges would give offenders a choice to go into the military; today, the military has certain standards that must be met, so "a" is not the best answer to this question.

85. A: Although the abuse of youthful offenders is rare, it has occurred, and critics often use this fact as an argument against boot camps used as form of punishment. A 16-year-old in Arizona died after intensive exercise, which some people argue is a common risk at boot camps. The potential for abuse is the most frequently cited criticism. Answer choices "b," "c," and "d" are either untrue or highly subjective.

86. D: Recidivism refers to convicts who commit new offenses after being released from prison for a prior offense. The rate of recidivism is often measured and cited as an evaluation of the effectiveness of rehabilitation programs.. The other answer choices may have some validity, but those choices are wrong because they do not reflect the specific meaning of the term "recidivism."

87. D: Different prisoners have different approaches to prison life. It is possible for a prisoner to serve "easy time" by following the rules and directions of the prison system. Other prisoners prefer to rebel continuously against prison authorities, and authorities generally react by strictly enforcing prison rules with these individuals. The concept is the same for short and longer term sentences and for the type of crimes committed, although child sex offenders are at significant risk in the prison environment. Choice "d" is the best answer.

88. D: Corrections officers are aware of prisoner's rights and know that respecting these rights is part of a successful prison institution. Prisoners are entitled to the rights expressed in answer choices "a," "b," and "c." However, answer "d" is the one we are looking for, as two hours of free time is NOT one of a prisoner's basic rights. The prison rules determine what hours an inmate may use for personal time, not the prisoners.

89. A: Prisoners are protected from "cruel and unusual punishment" by the Eighth Amendment to the US Constitution. The purpose of the Amendment is to prevent torture, abuse, and other forms of maltreatment, which could include encouraging other prisoners to assault the prisoner. The Second

Amendment applies generally to gun rights, the First Amendment pertains to free speech and religion, and the Fifth Amendment refers to protections against self-incrimination.

90. C: Penal system authorities may transfer prisoners for a variety of reasons, but it is a violation of a prisoner's rights to be transferred for reasons based on race, religion, or nationality. A prisoner's rights must always be respected, as indicated in answer choice "b," but that does not dictate whether or where a prisoner is transferred. Answer "d" may be true, but that in itself may not be a justification for moving a prisoner. Answer "a" is incorrect because there is no such law. The key idea is that prison authorities must have a non-discriminatory reason for transferring a prisoner.

91. D: The police officer was following procedure to seal off the area and let the shell casings lay where they were so that detectives or forensics personnel could work the scene. The officer's report will be very important, however, so it must be written as accurately as possible. The presence of shell casings and the type of wounds indicates that a pistol or rifle was used, making answer "d" the correct answer choice. Choice "b" would not be accurate because revolvers retain their shell casings after firing. Shotguns have different wound patterns and very different casings. Obviously, the screwdriver scenario would not be the best answer, given the presence of cartridge casings.

92. A: It is best just to know the meaning of terms and the way they are used in police training manuals. Answer "a" contains the correct meaning of both terms. A careful reading would show answer choice "d" to be nonsensical. Choice "b" simply reverses the meanings, and "c" is an answer designed to confuse the issue of patrolling techniques. Proactive patrols try to thwart crimes before they happen instead of reacting to crimes after the fact.

93. C: The phrase is Latin but it does not mean that the lawyer must speak Latin. In forma pauperis is not a welfare benefit, either, nor does it refer to rehabilitative services and probation. The correct answer is "c." The Latin phrase literally means "in the form of a pauper," and the US Constitution allows for the right to a free defense counsel and relief from court costs.

94. B: "Indictment" is one word that will appear regularly in all areas of law enforcement. An indictment is prepared by the prosecuting authority of the state, county, or federal investigative agency; therefore, "b" is the correct answer. Sometimes the indictment is prepared by a grand jury, but under no circumstances do police officers prepare an indictment. A criminal suspect may respond to an indictment by entering a plea, but the plea itself has a very different meaning than an indictment does.

95. A: Powell v. Alabama was a landmark case. The African American defendants, widely known as the "Scottsboro Boys," were accused of rape. Although they did have counsel representing them at trial, the lawyers were not provided until the proceedings were well under way, leaving them no time to prepare a defense. The court ruled that the defendants, who had been sentenced to death, had been deprived of due process.

96. D: Pre-trial diversion is a manner of disposing of a minor criminal case when the offender is not a habitual criminal. It is often applied to first-time offenders and is known by a variety of names in different states. Whatever term individual states may use, pre-trial diversion programs seek punishments that do not imprison the offender and are geared toward rehabilitation and giving the offender a "second chance." Under pre-trial diversion, an offender may be sentenced to community service and probation with monitoring. Choice "d" is the answer that best describes the "pre-trial diversion" process.

97. A: To answer this question correctly, one has to know the meaning of certain terms. "In forma pauperis" means that the suspect is a pauper and has the right to free counsel. All suspects "must" (not "may") have a fair trial—there is no "granting"—so choice "c" is incorrect. Excessively high bail is not a manifestation of the "innocent until proven guilty" idea. To answer the question, you have to know that being released on one's own "recognizance" means that a person presumed innocent can go home knowing he or she will have full freedom and rights unless later convicted.

98. C: The right to due process means that a criminal defendant and his attorney have the right to see and examine all evidence that the state holds against the accused. The prosecutors routinely send this information to the defense when they prepare their cases, but sometimes new evidence is found before the case goes to trial. To make sure they have it all, defense lawyers routinely file pre-trial discovery requests. "Discovery" means that the defense lawyer wants to "discover" all available evidence. Answer choice "c" is the best answer to this question.

99. D: The designation of "preventive detention" must be a careful one, but it is generally held to apply to dangerous terrorists and mentally ill people who are very likely to harm or kill others. Different countries have different definitions, conditions, and restrictions imposed upon preventive detention, but preventive detention is employed in the case of known dangerous terrorists and mentally ill people who have been judged likely to wound or kill other members of society. Answer "d" is the correct answer. Preventive detention extends the length of time a defendant can be held without charges or trial.

100. D: Auto stops and frisks are exceptions to search and seizure protections if these are conducted after or in the process of a "hot pursuit" apprehension, or if the search is related to a previous crime for which there is evidence of guilt. Airport and border searches are also exempted from search and seizure laws since the incidence of smuggling is likely, and the possibility of terrorism exists. Keep in mind that police chiefs cannot authorize search warrants under any conditions except for the one previously described, where the search may be conducted, in any case, by the patrol officer(s).

How to Overcome Test Anxiety

Just the thought of taking a test is enough to make most people a little nervous. A test is an important event that can have a long-term impact on your future, so it's important to take it seriously and it's natural to feel anxious about performing well. But just because anxiety is normal, that doesn't mean that it's helpful in test taking, or that you should simply accept it as part of your life. Anxiety can have a variety of effects. These effects can be mild, like making you feel slightly nervous, or severe, like blocking your ability to focus or remember even a simple detail.

If you experience test anxiety—whether severe or mild—it's important to know how to beat it. To discover this, first you need to understand what causes test anxiety.

Causes of Test Anxiety

While we often think of anxiety as an uncontrollable emotional state, it can actually be caused by simple, practical things. One of the most common causes of test anxiety is that a person does not feel adequately prepared for their test. This feeling can be the result of many different issues such as poor study habits or lack of organization, but the most common culprit is time management. Starting to study too late, failing to organize your study time to cover all of the material, or being distracted while you study will mean that you're not well prepared for the test. This may lead to cramming the night before, which will cause you to be physically and mentally exhausted for the test. Poor time management also contributes to feelings of stress, fear, and hopelessness as you realize you are not well prepared but don't know what to do about it.

Other times, test anxiety is not related to your preparation for the test but comes from unresolved fear. This may be a past failure on a test, or poor performance on tests in general. It may come from comparing yourself to others who seem to be performing better or from the stress of living up to expectations. Anxiety may be driven by fears of the future—how failure on this test would affect your educational and career goals. These fears are often completely irrational, but they can still negatively impact your test performance.

Elements of Test Anxiety

As mentioned earlier, test anxiety is considered to be an emotional state, but it has physical and mental components as well. Sometimes you may not even realize that you are suffering from test anxiety until you notice the physical symptoms. These can include trembling hands, rapid heartbeat, sweating, nausea, and tense muscles. Extreme anxiety may lead to fainting or vomiting. Obviously, any of these symptoms can have a negative impact on testing. It is important to recognize them as soon as they begin to occur so that you can address the problem before it damages your performance.

The mental components of test anxiety include trouble focusing and inability to remember learned information. During a test, your mind is on high alert, which can help you recall information and stay focused for an extended period of time. However, anxiety interferes with your mind's natural processes, causing you to blank out, even on the questions you know well. The strain of testing during anxiety makes it difficult to stay focused, especially on a test that may take several hours. Extreme anxiety can take a huge mental toll, making it difficult not only to recall test information but even to understand the test questions or pull your thoughts together.

Effects of Test Anxiety

Test anxiety is like a disease—if left untreated, it will get progressively worse. Anxiety leads to poor performance, and this reinforces the feelings of fear and failure, which in turn lead to poor performances on subsequent tests. It can grow from a mild nervousness to a crippling condition. If allowed to progress, test anxiety can have a big impact on your schooling, and consequently on your future.

Test anxiety can spread to other parts of your life. Anxiety on tests can become anxiety in any stressful situation, and blanking on a test can turn into panicking in a job situation. But fortunately, you don't have to let anxiety rule your testing and determine your grades. There are a number of relatively simple steps you can take to move past anxiety and function normally on a test and in the rest of life.

Physical Steps for Beating Test Anxiety

While test anxiety is a serious problem, the good news is that it can be overcome. It doesn't have to control your ability to think and remember information. While it may take time, you can begin taking steps today to beat anxiety.

Just as your first hint that you may be struggling with anxiety comes from the physical symptoms, the first step to treating it is also physical. Rest is crucial for having a clear, strong mind. If you are tired, it is much easier to give in to anxiety. But if you establish good sleep habits, your body and mind will be ready to perform optimally, without the strain of exhaustion. Additionally, sleeping well helps you to retain information better, so you're more likely to recall the answers when you see the test questions.

Getting good sleep means more than going to bed on time. It's important to allow your brain time to relax. Take study breaks from time to time so it doesn't get overworked, and don't study right before bed. Take time to rest your mind before trying to rest your body, or you may find it difficult to fall asleep.

Along with sleep, other aspects of physical health are important in preparing for a test. Good nutrition is vital for good brain function. Sugary foods and drinks may give a burst of energy but this burst is followed by a crash, both physically and emotionally. Instead, fuel your body with protein and vitamin-rich foods.

Also, drink plenty of water. Dehydration can lead to headaches and exhaustion, especially if your brain is already under stress from the rigors of the test. Particularly if your test is a long one, drink water during the breaks. And if possible, take an energy-boosting snack to eat between sections.

Along with sleep and diet, a third important part of physical health is exercise. Maintaining a steady workout schedule is helpful, but even taking 5-minute study breaks to walk can help get your blood pumping faster and clear your head. Exercise also releases endorphins, which contribute to a positive feeling and can help combat test anxiety.

When you nurture your physical health, you are also contributing to your mental health. If your body is healthy, your mind is much more likely to be healthy as well. So take time to rest, nourish your body with healthy food and water, and get moving as much as possible. Taking these physical steps will make you stronger and more able to take the mental steps necessary to overcome test anxiety.

Mental Steps for Beating Test Anxiety

Working on the mental side of test anxiety can be more challenging, but as with the physical side, there are clear steps you can take to overcome it. As mentioned earlier, test anxiety often stems from lack of preparation, so the obvious solution is to prepare for the test. Effective studying may be the most important weapon you have for beating test anxiety, but you can and should employ several other mental tools to combat fear.

First, boost your confidence by reminding yourself of past success—tests or projects that you aced. If you're putting as much effort into preparing for this test as you did for those, there's no reason you should expect to fail here. Work hard to prepare; then trust your preparation.

Second, surround yourself with encouraging people. It can be helpful to find a study group, but be sure that the people you're around will encourage a positive attitude. If you spend time with others who are anxious or cynical, this will only contribute to your own anxiety. Look for others who are motivated to study hard from a desire to succeed, not from a fear of failure.

Third, reward yourself. A test is physically and mentally tiring, even without anxiety, and it can be helpful to have something to look forward to. Plan an activity following the test, regardless of the outcome, such as going to a movie or getting ice cream.

When you are taking the test, if you find yourself beginning to feel anxious, remind yourself that you know the material. Visualize successfully completing the test. Then take a few deep, relaxing breaths and return to it. Work through the questions carefully but with confidence, knowing that you are capable of succeeding.

Developing a healthy mental approach to test taking will also aid in other areas of life. Test anxiety affects more than just the actual test—it can be damaging to your mental health and even contribute to depression. It's important to beat test anxiety before it becomes a problem for more than testing.

Study Strategy

Being prepared for the test is necessary to combat anxiety, but what does being prepared look like? You may study for hours on end and still not feel prepared. What you need is a strategy for test prep. The next few pages outline our recommended steps to help you plan out and conquer the challenge of preparation.

Step 1: Scope Out the Test

Learn everything you can about the format (multiple choice, essay, etc.) and what will be on the test. Gather any study materials, course outlines, or sample exams that may be available. Not only will this help you to prepare, but knowing what to expect can help to alleviate test anxiety.

Step 2: Map Out the Material

Look through the textbook or study guide and make note of how many chapters or sections it has. Then divide these over the time you have. For example, if a book has 15 chapters and you have five days to study, you need to cover three chapters each day. Even better, if you have the time, leave an extra day at the end for overall review after you have gone through the material in depth.

If time is limited, you may need to prioritize the material. Look through it and make note of which sections you think you already have a good grasp on, and which need review. While you are studying, skim quickly through the familiar sections and take more time on the challenging parts.

Write out your plan so you don't get lost as you go. Having a written plan also helps you feel more in control of the study, so anxiety is less likely to arise from feeling overwhelmed at the amount to cover.

Step 3: Gather Your Tools

Decide what study method works best for you. Do you prefer to highlight in the book as you study and then go back over the highlighted portions? Or do you type out notes of the important information? Or is it helpful to make flashcards that you can carry with you? Assemble the pens, index cards, highlighters, post-it notes, and any other materials you may need so you won't be distracted by getting up to find things while you study.

If you're having a hard time retaining the information or organizing your notes, experiment with different methods. For example, try color-coding by subject with colored pens, highlighters, or post-it notes. If you learn better by hearing, try recording yourself reading your notes so you can listen while in the car, working out, or simply sitting at your desk. Ask a friend to quiz you from your flashcards, or try teaching someone the material to solidify it in your mind.

Step 4: Create Your Environment

It's important to avoid distractions while you study. This includes both the obvious distractions like visitors and the subtle distractions like an uncomfortable chair (or a too-comfortable couch that makes you want to fall asleep). Set up the best study environment possible: good lighting and a comfortable work area. If background music helps you focus, you may want to turn it on, but otherwise keep the room quiet. If you are using a computer to take notes, be sure you don't have any other windows open, especially applications like social media, games, or anything else that could distract you. Silence your phone and turn off notifications. Be sure to keep water close by so you stay hydrated while you study (but avoid unhealthy drinks and snacks).

Also, take into account the best time of day to study. Are you freshest first thing in the morning? Try to set aside some time then to work through the material. Is your mind clearer in the afternoon or evening? Schedule your study session then. Another method is to study at the same time of day that you will take the test, so that your brain gets used to working on the material at that time and will be ready to focus at test time.

Step 5: Study!

Once you have done all the study preparation, it's time to settle into the actual studying. Sit down, take a few moments to settle your mind so you can focus, and begin to follow your study plan. Don't give in to distractions or let yourself procrastinate. This is your time to prepare so you'll be ready to fearlessly approach the test. Make the most of the time and stay focused.

Of course, you don't want to burn out. If you study too long you may find that you're not retaining the information very well. Take regular study breaks. For example, taking five minutes out of every hour to walk briskly, breathing deeply and swinging your arms, can help your mind stay fresh.

As you get to the end of each chapter or section, it's a good idea to do a quick review. Remind yourself of what you learned and work on any difficult parts. When you feel that you've mastered the material, move on to the next part. At the end of your study session, briefly skim through your notes again.

But while review is helpful, cramming last minute is NOT. If at all possible, work ahead so that you won't need to fit all your study into the last day. Cramming overloads your brain with more information than it can process and retain, and your tired mind may struggle to recall even previously learned information when it is overwhelmed with last-minute study. Also, the urgent nature of cramming and the stress placed on your brain contribute to anxiety. You'll be more likely to go to the test feeling unprepared and having trouble thinking clearly.

So don't cram, and don't stay up late before the test, even just to review your notes at a leisurely pace. Your brain needs rest more than it needs to go over the information again. In fact, plan to finish your studies by noon or early afternoon the day before the test. Give your brain the rest of the day to relax or focus on other things, and get a good night's sleep. Then you will be fresh for the test and better able to recall what you've studied.

STEP 6: TAKE A PRACTICE TEST

Many courses offer sample tests, either online or in the study materials. This is an excellent resource to check whether you have mastered the material, as well as to prepare for the test format and environment.

Check the test format ahead of time: the number of questions, the type (multiple choice, free response, etc.), and the time limit. Then create a plan for working through them. For example, if you have 30 minutes to take a 60-question test, your limit is 30 seconds per question. Spend less time on the questions you know well so that you can take more time on the difficult ones.

If you have time to take several practice tests, take the first one open book, with no time limit. Work through the questions at your own pace and make sure you fully understand them. Gradually work up to taking a test under test conditions: sit at a desk with all study materials put away and set a timer. Pace yourself to make sure you finish the test with time to spare and go back to check your answers if you have time.

After each test, check your answers. On the questions you missed, be sure you understand why you missed them. Did you misread the question (tests can use tricky wording)? Did you forget the information? Or was it something you hadn't learned? Go back and study any shaky areas that the practice tests reveal.

Taking these tests not only helps with your grade, but also aids in combating test anxiety. If you're already used to the test conditions, you're less likely to worry about it, and working through tests until you're scoring well gives you a confidence boost. Go through the practice tests until you feel comfortable, and then you can go into the test knowing that you're ready for it.

Test Tips

On test day, you should be confident, knowing that you've prepared well and are ready to answer the questions. But aside from preparation, there are several test day strategies you can employ to maximize your performance.

First, as stated before, get a good night's sleep the night before the test (and for several nights before that, if possible). Go into the test with a fresh, alert mind rather than staying up late to study.

Try not to change too much about your normal routine on the day of the test. It's important to eat a nutritious breakfast, but if you normally don't eat breakfast at all, consider eating just a protein bar. If you're a coffee drinker, go ahead and have your normal coffee. Just make sure you time it so that the caffeine doesn't wear off right in the middle of your test. Avoid sugary beverages, and drink enough water to stay hydrated but not so much that you need a restroom break 10 minutes into the test. If your test isn't first thing in the morning, consider going for a walk or doing a light workout before the test to get your blood flowing.

Allow yourself enough time to get ready, and leave for the test with plenty of time to spare so you won't have the anxiety of scrambling to arrive in time. Another reason to be early is to select a good seat. It's helpful to sit away from doors and windows, which can be distracting. Find a good seat, get out your supplies, and settle your mind before the test begins.

When the test begins, start by going over the instructions carefully, even if you already know what to expect. Make sure you avoid any careless mistakes by following the directions.

Then begin working through the questions, pacing yourself as you've practiced. If you're not sure on an answer, don't spend too much time on it, and don't let it shake your confidence. Either skip it and come back later, or eliminate as many wrong answers as possible and guess among the remaining ones. Don't dwell on these questions as you continue—put them out of your mind and focus on what lies ahead.

Be sure to read all of the answer choices, even if you're sure the first one is the right answer. Sometimes you'll find a better one if you keep reading. But don't second-guess yourself if you do immediately know the answer. Your gut instinct is usually right. Don't let test anxiety rob you of the information you know.

If you have time at the end of the test (and if the test format allows), go back and review your answers. Be cautious about changing any, since your first instinct tends to be correct, but make sure you didn't misread any of the questions or accidentally mark the wrong answer choice. Look over any you skipped and make an educated guess.

At the end, leave the test feeling confident. You've done your best, so don't waste time worrying about your performance or wishing you could change anything. Instead, celebrate the successful completion of this test. And finally, use this test to learn how to deal with anxiety even better next time.

Review Video: Test Anxiety
Visit mometrix.com/academy and enter code: 100340

Important Qualification

Not all anxiety is created equal. If your test anxiety is causing major issues in your life beyond the classroom or testing center, or if you are experiencing troubling physical symptoms related to your anxiety, it may be a sign of a serious physiological or psychological condition. If this sounds like your situation, we strongly encourage you to seek professional help.

Online Resources

Due to our efforts to try to keep this book to a manageable length, we've created a link that will give you access to all of your online resources:

mometrix.com/resources719/dsstcrimjust

It's Your Moment, Let's Celebrate It!

Share your story @mometrixtestpreparation